Listening *for* heaven's sake

Building Healthy Relationships With God, Self and Others

Dr. Gary Sweeten
Dave Ping & Anne Clippard

APPLES OF GOLD SERIES • BOOK ONE

First Edition, November, 1993

Cover design by Lois Dunn
Photo courtesy of Audrey D. Boettcher

Library of Congress Cataloging-in-Publication Data

Sweeten, Gary R., 1938—
Ping, Dave & Clippard, Anne
   Listening for heaven's sake
   Building Healthy Relationships With God, Self and Others
   —Apples of Gold Series - Book One

ISBN: 0-9638518-1-0 paper
ISBN: 0-9638518-0-2 cloth

208   V 1   93-61305
                                                     CIP

This edition published by Teleios Publications,
4015 Executive Park Drive, Suite 309 Cincinnati, Ohio 45241
(513) 769-5353

96 97 / 10 9 8 7 6 5 4 3
Printed and bound in the United States of America.

Acknowledgments

The poet Homer said, "Light is the task where many share the toil." We would like to express our deepest gratitude for the loving toil of the many friends who labored along with us to bring this book into being.

It would be impossible to adequately acknowledge all of the individuals who ultimately made this new edition possible. However, we would like to give special thanks to our good friend Rose Huber for her priceless assistance both in writing and in editing. Rose helped breathe vitality and life into our material with new illustrations, stories and examples. Lois Dunn helped greatly with the graphics and layout of the book. Karen Carter, Julia Sweeten Knisple, Pam Ping, Bob and Scotti Hammond, and Terry Baker also deserve special thanks for their painstaking work in typing, proofreading and editing.

Furthermore, we thank all the EMI teachers and facilitators for donating countless hours testing and improving these materials over the years. We especially recognize the wonderful contribution of the leadership and the congregation of College Hill Presbyterian Church in nurturing and developing the seeds that eventually yielded the fruit you see in these pages. Thanks belong to Dr. Richard Walters and Dr. James Kallas for providing much of the inspiration and many of the key insights put forward in this volume.

A special word of thanks also belongs to the therapists, counselors and wounded healers of LIFE WAY Christian Counseling who have used these materials to bring hope, healing and renewal to so many hurting people.

We thank God for the opportunity to share these Apples of Gold with you. We pray that the Holy Spirit will empower our simple words to your benefit.

Gary R. Sweeten
David W. Ping
Anne T. Clippard

July 1993

Table of Illustrations

*T*able *of* *C*ontents

Preface

It's probably no accident that you've picked up this book.

- Perhaps the title intrigued you.

- Perhaps a friend recommended it to you.

- Perhaps a *still small voice* reminded you that you need to work on developing greater intimacy in your friendships or with your spouse and children.

Whatever drew you to it, consider that it may be God's distinctive way of leading you toward healthier, more fulfilling relationships. Many individuals from widely different cultural, religious and social backgrounds have asserted that their encounter with the ideas contained in this volume have helped them to grow closer to God and others in a completely fresh way.

That's our goal: to help you experience more of the abundant life promised to us in John 10:10 when Jesus said, "I am come that they might have life, and that they might have it more abundantly" (KJV).

Although uncommonly rich in material goods, we in the western world often suffer from poverty in the area of quality relationships. Hectic schedules, broken families, social pressures and frequent mobility rob us of many of the inner riches God intends for His people. If social science researchers are correct, the downward spiral of unhealthy, indifferent and destructive relationships is nearing a crisis point in our society.

A study by the U.S. Census Bureau comparing the United States with other developed countries presents alarming evidence of family and relational fragmentation. Since the 1980s our country has had:

- The highest divorce rate in the world, 64% higher than any other country studied.
- The highest percentage of children raised by a single parent.
- The highest teen pregnancy rates in the world.
- The highest percentage of violent deaths among youth.
- A homicide rate that is five times higher than that of any other developed country except Mexico.[1]

We also see increases in the number of families suffering from the effects of depression, alcoholism, physical or sexual abuse, and a wide range of other serious relational problems.

None of us is immune to these disturbing trends — not even the most caring Christian. They touch us personally in many ways. They touch our families, our churches, our businesses and our friends. Now as never before, hurting people are looking to the Church to provide a place of healing and refuge. In an ever deepening hunger for health, Christians are seeking practical help from pastors, counselors and support groups. Yet few churches have the resources, the programs or the personnel to provide meaningful support to all of those seeking help.

Many churches are already overwhelmed by the flood of people coming to them for help with difficult emotional issues. The startling increase in individual and family dysfunction has forced many to reevaluate their approach to counseling within the Church. There is a growing realization that it's time to turn back to Scripture for a better model, one that looks to the community and the church rather than to the pastor or to "expert" counselors alone.

Scripture's emphasis on the ministry or "priesthood" of all believers leads us to the conclusion that high quality caring and support at home, at work and at church provide the key to mental, emotional and spiritual health. Scripture contains the power and insight to "heal the broken-hearted" and to "set the captives free" (Isaiah 61:1). God encourages us to integrate His love, truth and power into our own lives as well as in ministry to others.

What's In It For Me?

Even if you aren't interested in counseling or theology, there is something here for you. If you are tired of unsatisfying or mediocre relationships and would like to relate more helpfully with others, this is the book for you! *Listening for heaven's sake* is designed to help you to deepen and improve *all* of your relationships. Whether you're a single person searching for friendship, a spouse desiring to strengthen your marriage, a parent wishing to improve communication with your children, a counselor wanting to help your clients overcome problems, a manager seeking to become more effective in team building, a teacher trying to relate better with your students — no matter what your occupation or stage of life — the concepts and practical skills contained in this book can help you.

This is not an ordinary self-help book. It's not meant to be read and then put back on the shelf. It's meant to be lived out in your daily relationships. The information, techniques and practical exercises contained here have been carefully crafted to help you grow in skills we have christened the "art of heavenly listening." By understanding and applying these skills, you can deepen your understanding of yourself, improve your ability to relate effectively with others, and strengthen your personal relationship with God.

Apples of Gold

Most of the material you'll be reading in this book has its roots in Dr. Gary Sweeten's research. In 1975, Gary completed a doctoral dissertation aimed at developing a systematic skill training program for pastors and lay people.[2] His goal was, and continues to be, to discover the best methods for empowering Christians to grow personally and to become more effective in ministering health and life to others.

During 16 years serving on the pastoral staff of College Hill Presbyterian Church, he refined his theories and put them into practice, training the pastoral staff and several thousand lay people in essential relationship and ministry skills. As the training impacted lives, the congregation experienced tremendous healing and growth.

The introductory training course was entitled *Apples of Gold* referring to Proverbs 25 :11 — "A word aptly spoken is like apples of gold in settings of silver."

Word of our *Apples* training soon spread to lay people, missionaries and pastors from many other congregations. They began attending workshops and then reproducing our model in their home settings. Gary's experience and research as a professional counselor, combined with the insights and expertise of many others who have used our training model, have resulted in a series of courses that bring new life to churches.

Listening for heaven's sake is the first part of our *Apples of Gold* training series and our primary course in caring and listening skills. It serves as a foundation for all of our *Teleios* courses including: *Apples of Gold II[3], Rational Christian Thinking[4], Breaking Free from the Past[5],* and *Christian Family Systems[6].*

The original *Apples of Gold I[7]* material has been rewritten and revised many times over the years by several dedicated teachers and professional people who have used this material and have been blessed by it. The current edition has been substantially expanded by David Ping and Anne Clippard, two of our most experienced instructors. It now includes more of the biblical, theological and theoretical basis of our teaching and provides more in-depth coverage of the practical skills involved in becoming a healthier and more compassionate listener.

To make the information more interesting and readable, we have adopted a more informal style. Wherever possible, we have illustrated with true first-person stories. Although Gary is the narrator of many of these accounts, they have been compiled from the experiences of various individuals.

How You'll Benefit From This Book

Since 1977, people across the country and around the world have used the ideas, skills and techniques presented in this book to experience new life and wholeness.

They report learning a variety of practical life-changing HOW TOs including:

- How to listen with greater insight and understanding.
- How to improve compassion and friendliness toward others.
- How to develop more self-respect and greater respect for others.
- How to embrace a more accurate sense of self-worth.
- How to avoid codependent relationships and compassion burnout.
- How to improve conflicted relationships.
- How to enhance communication with spouse and children.
- How to empower others to work together with greater effectiveness.
- How to experience more of God's love and the fruit of the Spirit.

Growing the Fruit of the Spirit

Our desire for you as you read and apply the principles contained in the next several chapters is that you will discover how to grow more of the fruit of the Spirit in your life.

> *But the fruit of the Spirit is love, joy, peace, patience, kindness, goodness, faithfulness, gentleness and self-control. . .* (Galatians 5:22, 23)

You're probably quite familiar with this passage, but have you ever considered how to grow these qualities in your life or what they would look like in your relationships?

We will endeavor to give you a picture of healthy growth and a feasible process for experiencing more of the good fruit in your life. Most of us experience plenty of unhealthy or rotten fruit in our relationships already. We would like to grow more peaceful, joyful, loving, patient, etc. The chart on the next page pictures the process of moving from unwholesome or "wormy" fruit to the wholesome and nourishing fruit of the Holy Spirit.

Wouldn't it be wonderful to experience more of the good fruit?

It's interesting that the qualities listed in Galatians 5:22, 23 closely parallel the characteristics we observe in effective listeners and genuinely caring individuals. We have discovered over the years that when we help people develop sound listening, communication and caring skills based on Christ-centered teaching, they also experience dramatic growth in the fruit of the Spirit.

Scripture and experience teach us that a dynamic process of healing and growing involves receiving God's *truth* through the Scriptures, renewing our lives and relationships with the *fruit* of the Spirit, and using the *gifts* of the Spirit to minister life to others. We hope you will benefit from the fruit of our labors and enjoy the process of learning the art of *Listening for heaven's sake.*

> Gary R. Sweeten
> David W. Ping
> Anne T. Clippard

GROWING HEALTHY FRUIT

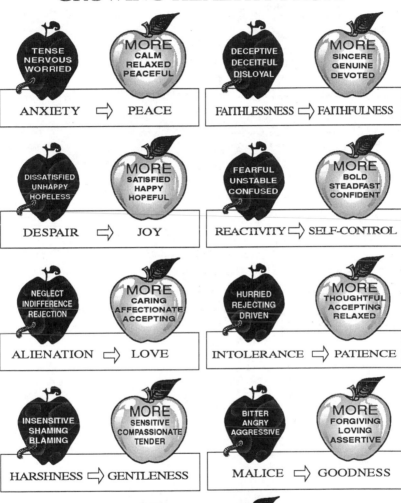

ANXIETY ⇨ PEACE

FAITHLESSNESS ⇨ FAITHFULNESS

DESPAIR ⇨ JOY

REACTIVITY ⇨ SELF-CONTROL

ALIENATION ⇨ LOVE

INTOLERANCE ⇨ PATIENCE

HARSHNESS ⇨ GENTLENESS

MALICE ⇨ GOODNESS

SELFISHNESS ⇨ KINDNESS

*I*ntroduction

In the spring of 1930, 9-year-old Anna Marie found herself on a ship bound for America, "the land of opportunity." She was going to meet her father, Antonio, who had emigrated from his native Italy to pave the way for his family.

With the young girl were her mother, her sister, an aunt and three cousins. All had left their small peasant village near Naples knowing they would never again see many of their relatives, including Anna Marie's grandparents who had encouraged Antonio to seek a better life for his wife and two daughters.

In the middle of their 12-day voyage across the Atlantic, the ship battled its way through a violent storm. Life jackets were issued; and the frightened passengers huddled together, praying for safety. Today, more than 60 years later, 73-year-old Anna Marie recalls the traumatic journey as if it all happened yesterday:

> *We were all so scared. But Mom, she was always so strong. I remember her holding me and my sister close to her and saying, "God will take care of us. He is with us. He touches us all the time — if we let Him. Here, take my hand," she added, squeezing my sister's hand and mine in hers. "This isn't just me holding your hand. God is touching you, too. He works through each of us. Now, you pass it on. You hold Maria's hand.*

> *And Maria, you hold Tony's hand. God will give*
> *us all strength through His Holy Spirit."*

Anna Marie's story beautifully expresses an idea embodied in two Greek words used throughout the New Testament: *teleios,* which means growth into wholeness and Christian maturity, and *paraklesis,* which means "to draw near" another person to provide comfort, encouragement, exhortation and counsel.

Second Corinthians 1:4 tells us that God "comforts us in all our troubles, so that we can comfort [paraklesis] those in any trouble with the comfort we ourselves have received from God."

Anna Marie's mother modeled the New Testament idea of *paraklesis* by drawing her children near and comforting them with the faith and hope she herself received from God. In her simple wisdom, she knew that God's comfort, encouragement and help are meant to be passed on.

God helps us grow healthier, happier and more complete in our own lives and then he uses us to bring more wholeness into the lives of others. But the process doesn't stop there. Like the miraculous loaves and fishes, our health and wholeness only increase as we give to others.

Just as Anna Marie's mother drew close to her family as a helper, sharing faith and comfort in the midst of a difficult situation, our goal in this book is to help you become healthier **parakletes** and, therefore, healthier people. By growing in Christian maturity ourselves (*teleios*) and caring for others in healthy ways (*paraklesis*), we will be able to experience the abundant life that is ours by birthright and by God's promise.

Making Your D.R.E.A.M.S. Come True

Our desire, then, is to give you a simple method for growing into *teleios* and becoming a better *paraklete*. In so doing, we believe we can help make your dreams of healthy, fulfilling relationships become reality.

As you incorporate the principles of *teleios* and *paraklesis* into your day-to-day living, you'll probably find that you have a clearer insight into yourself and those around you. You may even realize that you've removed some of the clutter from your life so that you can move ahead with your personal goals, your hopes for your family, your professional life and your dreams.

In fact, you'll find that D.R.E.A.M.S. play a major role in our teaching methodology. It's an approach we've found to be very effective in our seminars over the years. Broken down, the acrostic translates:

• *Didactic*. Derived from the Greek work *didaktikos*, didactic means "skilled teaching." The information is presented to us and we absorb it. Studying and learning relational skills requires understanding factual research and spiritual concepts. Both research data (including findings from professional literature) and Scriptural lessons will be presented in this book. But information alone won't produce lasting changes.

• *Reflection*. As difficult as it is for many of us to find "quiet time" in our hurried schedules, thinking about what we've read is important because it increases our depth of learning. In fact, it's essential if we're going to develop any depth of understanding and insight into ourselves and others. *Selah!* is a Hebrew word used in the Psalms that encourages readers to "pause and think." Throughout this book, we encourage you to take time to reflect.

• *Experience*. Knowledge and information are more often *caught* than *taught*. I believe that knowledge separated from experience always remains in the realm of doubt. We hope you will take the information from these pages and put it into practice in your life. Experience really *is* the best teacher.

• *Accountability*. There's an old management axiom that says, "People tend to do what you *inspect* and not what you *expect*." There's some truth to that. Accountability allows us to track our progress and improve our effectiveness. As you practice the skills presented here, ask a friend to help by holding you accountable for becoming a better helper and a more effective listener.

• *Modeling.* This is simply a matter of watching others who are more skilled than you are and imitating their techniques — rather like an apprenticeship program. Just like the old days when kids had real heroes to emulate. Paul the Apostle encouraged his listeners to "follow my example, as I follow the example of Christ" (1 Cor. 11:1).

• *Spiritual.* We learn best when we invite God, through the Holy Spirit, to teach and empower us. As James 1:5 tells us, "If any of you lacks wisdom, he should ask God, who gives generously to all without finding fault, and it will be given to him." God delights in developing the fruit of the Spirit in our lives.

A New Life in the Spirit

The D.R.E.A.M.S. acrostic reminds me of Anna Marie's father and the many immigrants like him who paved the way for a new life for their families.

After landing on our shores they had to learn a new language and absorb a radically different culture. They had plenty to reflect on. They learned to adapt through practical experiences (and, yes, through mistakes). They held one another accountable for their actions and decisions. And they gravitated toward real life models and mentors who helped ease their difficult transition to a whole new way of living.

As Anna Marie's vivid memories indicate, many such immigrants accomplished all of this with powerful, supernatural help from God.

It's my hope and prayer that as you learn the art of *Listening for heaven's sake,* it will become a way of living for you and for those you hold most dear — for all, in fact, whose lives you touch.

An Invitation to Healthy Living

Think of this book as a personal invitation to experience more health and fulfillment in your relationship with God, with yourself and with other people.

No matter what your temperament or talents, no matter what life experiences have brought you this far, you can learn to improve your relationships by using the skills that you will learn in the following chapters.

Over the years that we've been teaching these skills around the world in our LIFE Seminars, thousands of lay people and professionals have learned to enhance their interpersonal relationship and ministry skills. Marty, an elementary school teacher who attended one of our recent workshops, is a good example.

Marty came convinced that she would never be able to truly relate effectively with other people. "I'm not naturally gifted for this sort of thing," she confided during a break. "I've never felt really close to anyone. I don't even relate very well with my students."

After practicing the skills you will be studying in this book, Marty was elated. "Now I know I can change!" she shared with excitement. "For the first time, I have tools to work on unhealthy areas of my life. It's exciting for me to realize that I can learn how to have healthy relationships."

Like so many others who have taken part in our LIFE Seminars over the years, Marty's experience was life changing.

So was Daryl's. A denominational pastor, Daryl assumed that he had read enough of the Bible, taken enough courses and digested enough self-help books to be an expert listener. "Then I took a LIFE Seminar," he told us.

> *I expected a beginners' workshop—a review of things I had already learned elsewhere. But the seminar brought me to my knees. Suddenly I became aware of the depth and breadth that Christian relationships can attain. I, a 'good listener,' realized that by being silent I hadn't always been listening, hadn't always cared about the other person. And, as a 'mature' Christian, I always had a good answer ready for people with problems — even when I didn't try to understand the question first.*

Daryl also told us how the principles you will learn in the following pages helped him to overcome blind spots that blocked him as he sought to apply practical biblical principles in his ministry. "I still have far to go. There have been times since that first seminar when my mettle has been tested like never before, but God has prepared me for it, and I am thankful."

Doug, another LIFE Seminar participant, says that once he incorporated what he learned into his life, even his physical health improved. As a child of an abusive alcoholic family, Doug talked openly of his own use of drugs as a teenager and about his emotional estrangement from his family.

> *Once I learned to communicate with others in healthier ways, my anxiety level went down substantially. That has had a positive ripple effect on my marriage and on every other area of my life. I am much less vulnerable to depression and, amazingly, I have fewer colds, headaches and stomach problems than before.*

As you can see, healthy living and caring skills can help you in many different areas of your life. As Doug told us:

> *Everyone goofs up. The key is knowing what to do about it. People today want straightforward information about how to improve their lives. We don't want a lot of psychological double-talk. These techniques are real and usable by the average human being. Best of all, they really work!*

We hope that you, like Marty, Daryl and Doug, will experience the many physical, emotional and spiritual rewards of healthier living.

Chasing Happiness

Have you ever wondered how to find health and happiness? You're certainly not alone. Since the moment Adam and Eve left the Garden of Eden, humankind has been on a desperate search for the peaceful state of being that was our original birthright.

The book of Ecclesiastes documents one of history's most systematic pursuers of happiness. The author, you might recall, tried unsuccessfully to find happiness through fame and wealth, wisdom and knowledge, political power and hard work. He sampled all the pleasures that wine, women and song could provide. But King Solomon was still frustrated and unfulfilled. In despair, he bitterly complained that trying to find happiness is like "chasing after the wind" (Ecclesiastes 2:11).

For generations, people have been trying to find genuine happiness by pursuing temporary pleasures. Advertisers constantly play on our hunger for happiness by trying to convince us that a new car, a designer wardrobe or even a particular brand of aftershave will provide the key to satisfaction. The *cosmedicine* industry (a late 20th century blend of medicine and cosmetology) markets the idea that changing our physical appearance will do the trick. If the recent boom in the cosmetic surgery industry is any indication, modern society has yet to learn the 3,000-year-old lesson of Ecclesiastes — that externals such as money, appearance, fame and good fortune (enjoyable as they might be) are not the keys to *long-term* happiness.

Remember Howard Hughes? At age 45 he was one of the richest and most flamboyant men in the world. He courted famous actresses, piloted exotic test aircraft, and owned a global airline and a worldwide string of hotels.

By age 65 Hughes was the world's richest man, but his life was a horror few of us can begin to imagine. He lived in seclusion without friendship or sunlight. His powerful six-foot-four body had shrunk to under 100 pounds. His once handsome features were hidden by a waist-length mass of tangled beard and hair, and his fingernails had grown to more than two inches in length. Addicted to drugs and deathly afraid of germs, the billionaire eventually died miserable and alone.

Howard Hughes is a good illustration of the findings reported in a recent *USA Today* piece called "What is Happiness?"[1] Researcher Roger F. Englehart writes that despite all their advantages, the wealthy report no more satisfaction in their lives than do the poor. There is, on the contrary, ample evidence that fame and fortune often end in misery. Besides Howard Hughes, consider Judy Garland, Marilyn Monroe, Elvis Presley, Karen Carpenter and John Belushi — people who seemed to "have it all." All engaged in self-destructive behaviors that ultimately robbed them of their happiness, peace and joy.

Contrary, then, to what popular culture teaches, pleasure and happiness are not synonymous. While life presents many opportunities for momentary pleasures and happy moments, long-term happiness usually requires an arduous process of growth and development.

What's Healthy?

If happiness is difficult to find, trying to determine what's healthy can be downright perplexing. Just ask the question, "What is a healthy relationship?" and, depending on who you're talking to, you're bound to get a wide variety of answers. Even the "experts" contradict each other more often than they agree.

In my personal and professional quest to discover the secrets of health and happiness, I've come to see that King Solomon was right all along. After trying all the possibilities, he concluded that without healthy relationships with God and others, everything else is "meaningless under the sun." In other words, wealth, power and prestige are worthless without the divine and human relationships that truly make life rich. As a business leader once told me, "I make a good living, but it's my family and friends who make living worthwhile." The things I learned in Sunday school about loving God, others and myself have been confirmed and proven by research and personal experience.

Solomon points to the vital role of caring relationships when he says in Ecclesiastes 4:9, 10, 12b:

> *Two are better than one, because they have a good return for their work: If one falls down, his friend can help him up. But pity the man who falls and has no one to help him up! ... A cord of three strands cannot easily be broken.*

This is a marvelous foreshadowing of Matthew 22:36-40. Do you remember the story? A lawyer went to Jesus and asked, "Teacher, which is the greatest commandment in the Law?"

Jesus replied: "'Love the Lord your God with all your heart and with all your soul and with all your mind' [Deuteronomy 6:5]. This is the first and greatest commandment."

Jesus didn't stop there, however. He continued: "And the second is like it: 'Love your neighbor as yourself' [Leviticus 19:18]." Then He summed it up by saying, "All the Law and the Prophets hang on these two commandments."

Do you see the three strands?

First, as human beings our health and happiness depend on a loving relationship with God, our heavenly Father. The second strand of health and happiness requires loving relationships with the people around us. The third and final strand is clear: if we are to have quality love for others, we must obviously have love for ourselves as well.

As a believing Christian and a professional counselor, I have discovered that health and happiness depend on balance in our relationships — with God, others and ourselves. To visualize what I am talking about, imagine a modified carpenter's level with three windows. The central window represents our relationship with God; the left-hand window represents our relationships with others; and the right-hand window shows our relationship to self.

If, for instance, my life is out of balance in the direction of self-centeredness, willfulness or narcissism, my other relationships will also suffer. I can't be completely self-focused and maintain healthy relationships with God and others, for when I am excessively wrapped up with myself, all other aspects of my life will be unhealthy and out of balance.

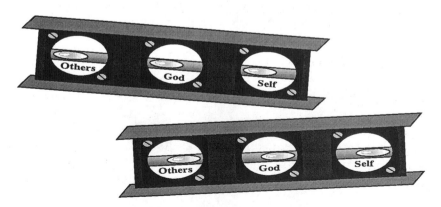

On the other hand, when my life is out of balance in the direction of people-pleasing, the result is similar. A life overly focused on meeting the needs and desires of others at the expense of my relationship with God and of my own identity as His child can be as unhealthy as self-centeredness. As the title of Dr. Margaret Rinck's book *Can Christians Love Too Much?* implies, we *can* love inappropriately.[2] (More on this later.)

First John 4:19-21 offers another view on the same principles. "We love because He [God] first loved us." God's love for us makes it possible for us to relate lovingly and healthfully toward others and toward ourselves. "If anyone says, 'I love God,' yet hates his brother, he is a liar. For anyone who does not love his brother, whom he has seen, cannot love God, whom he has not seen."

Many modern health care experts are excited to discover the mind-body connections in health. However, the psalmist saw this connection hundreds of years ago. Reflect for a moment on Psalm 32:3 (RSV): "When I declared not my sin, my body wasted away."

The whole Judeo-Christian tradition is the fount from which ancient and modern health care sprang. Hebrew priests were the first community health officials who, as directed by God, developed the standards for disease control, mental health, and marriage and family functioning. By the way, Jesus is known as the Great Physician; and James tells us to "confess our sins to one another and pray for one another that you may be healed" (James 5:16 [RSV]). All this shows the unity of the person in search for health.

The Whole Picture

Interestingly enough, our modern English words for *health*, *wholeness* and *holiness* are each related to the same Old English root word *hāl*. Clearly, our ancestors accepted a more unified and complete picture of health that encompassed our relationship to God and others along with physical well-being. In more recent history, however, scholars have sought to understand the secrets of health and happiness through *dividing* their studies into particular disciplines. Philosophers, theologians, biologists, anthropologists and psychologists now generally look at health from distinctly different perspectives.

The medical disciplines, for example, focus primarily on the body and the physical aspects of health. A medical doctor usually takes heredity, biochemistry, physiology, nutrition and diet into account to determine whether we're healthy or "normal." Our blood pressure, heart rate, body temperature and immune responses provide clues to whether our body is functioning properly.

The psychological disciplines, on the other hand, traditionally focus on the mental, emotional and behavioral aspects of health. A psychologist or counselor usually looks at how we deal with thoughts, feelings, decisions, relationships, stress and trauma. Our anxiety level, defenses, coping mechanisms, self-esteem and relational effectiveness (or lack thereof) provide clues to determine whether we're emotionally or mentally healthy.

Theological disciplines have, as a rule, concerned themselves with the spiritual and moral aspects of our lives — such as faith, hope, love, free will and sin. Christian ministers, preachers and theologians seek to help us develop a healthy relationship with God and others by helping us understand, interpret and apply biblical principles to our lives.

If we are to develop a balanced picture of what's healthy, this question naturally arises: *Is it the medical, the psychological or the theological discipline that is most important?*

The answer is. . . a resounding "Yes!"

In terms of overall health, the three disciplines are indivisible. We simply can't separate or leave any of them out and have a helpful, integrated picture of health.

Unfortunately, until recently most approaches to developing healthy relationships have included only one or two dimensions. They have relied solely on psychology or medicine and haven't even attempted to address the spiritual dimensions of life. Conversely, many Christians are openly antagonistic to the medical and psychological disciplines. Over the years, I've learned that this is not only shortsighted, but it's also not biblical, as we have just seen.

"It's of the Devil"

When I began studying counseling from a professional perspective, I returned to my home church in southern Illinois for a visit. It didn't take long for some of the older folks there to warn me about my professional pursuits.

"Stay away from that counseling stuff, Gary Ray," they chastised. "It's of the devil!" I had to chuckle to myself. Many of my secular colleagues had given me the exact opposite warning. As far as they were concerned, anything having to do with Christianity or the Bible was "of the devil" because they believed it was bound up in superstition and unreality.

Who Should I Believe?

As a Bible-believing Christian, I saw many errors in the basic assumptions of my secular teachers and fellow researchers. But they also had many good ideas, sound theories and techniques that could help people in the Church to live healthier, fuller lives. I had to find a way to bring good helping techniques together with solid biblical teachings. Since that time, I've relied on three basic assumptions to determine what is healthy and balanced.

• My first assumption is that **the supernatural tenets of orthodox Christianity are true**. The incarnation, virgin birth, miracles and the resurrection of Jesus were real events. The Scriptures provide me with a true revelation that can help me understand God and live more effectively day to day. They tell me of Christ's death and resurrection and how I can have a personal relationship with God. This is supernatural or "special revelation."

In light of this assumption, I believe the psychological and counseling sciences are like X-rays. They can provide assessment *tools* to figure out what is wrong, but they *can't* provide real, in-depth healing without God's truth and power.

• My second assumption is that **Jesus is the Lord of all life**. All things in heaven and earth were created and are sustained by Him. Studying any aspect of creation, then, reveals truth that can be useful to me as I seek to grow in health and understanding. So I don't have to be afraid of honest scientific inquiry; it will only lead me to a deeper understanding of both the creation and the Creator. This is the "natural revelation" referred to by Paul in Romans 1:20: "For since the creation of the world God's invisible qualities—His eternal power and divine nature—have been clearly seen, being understood from what has been made . . ."

This truth demands that I seek to understand God's creation in order to discover His revelation through nature. For believers, this includes the acceptance and use of medicine, counseling, mathematics and the other "ologies" . . . including theology, the study of God.

• My third assumption is that as a Christian, **I am called to use the best of research and scholarship available in my search for truth**. Christian principles, then, guide all of my efforts as a professional counselor and not simply those activities considered "sacred." There is no true "sacred/ secular" split in life. As a Christian, I have no hesitation in studying medicine, psychology or any other science in the search for truth. I can learn a great deal from what both Christian and non-Christian researchers discover, but I must responsibly measure both against biblical standards.

These three assumptions allow me to fearlessly test any information, theory or study to determine its value. As a Christian who desires to be healthy myself and to help others, I'm interested in growing and learning more about God through both His Scripture and His creation.

In this pursuit to grow in knowledge and in the Spirit, I've concluded that if we're grounded in solid biblical assumptions, we can freely evaluate and utilize scientific research and helping methods. This fits in well with my basic premise that a balanced understanding of health and happiness depends on a God-centered view of ourselves and others.

Of course, once I have a picture of what a balanced or healthy relationship is intended to look like, I will be better prepared to deal with the dysfunction and complex problems that afflict human beings. In the next chapter, we'll look at the source of problems and a plan for ministry to the people who are afflicted by them.

It's All Grace, Folks!

Just about everybody I know *is* a problem, *has* a problem or *lives with* a problem.

Unfortunately, most of our problems don't have simple black-and-white answers. More often than not, they're confusing and multifaceted.

Barbara's Story

To illustrate, I'd like to tell you about a friend named Barbara. When Barbara first came to our church, her life was, in her own words, "a mess."

She and her husband Tom had been married 21 years. They had three daughters — ages 17, 13 and 9.

In the weeks prior to our meeting, Barbara had been tested for just about every physical ailment you could name. She had chronic headaches and frequent fainting spells. Her heart would race out of control and she often felt dizzy. After in-depth testing for everything from menopause to brain tumors, she was given a clean bill of health, physically. The diagnosis: *anxiety*.

Barbara certainly seemed to have plenty to be anxious about. Her 17-year-old daughter was pregnant and unmarried. Raised as a devout Christian, Barbara had always tried to live by the highest moral standards and to pass those standards on to her children. When her daughter Melissa fell short of her expectations, Barbara was devastated and blamed herself. To make things worse, her husband also blamed her for the pregnancy, claiming that she had given their daughter too much freedom with the boyfriend (a young man he had always despised).

Even though she understood intellectually that it was Melissa's own choices that led to the situation, Barbara continued to carry a burden of intense shame believing she had failed as a Christian mother. Eventually these inner churnings manifested themselves in very real, physical symptoms.

The snowball effect intensified further, eroding the family dynamics in many even more negative ways.

Melissa's younger sisters, for example, began acting out their frustrations and confused feelings, adding to the tension in their household. The 13-year-old, who had always been a straight-A student, began bringing home failing grades; she refused to do any homework. She even got into a fight with another student, an action that was very much out of character for her.

The youngest daughter, who had always struggled with a weight problem, buried her misery in food — gaining more weight and becoming the brunt of unkind jokes and jeers from her peers. Soon she was developing stomachaches every morning in an attempt to stay home from school.

Meanwhile, Barbara and Tom's marriage slowly began to crumble. They couldn't discuss any of the family issues because they would always end up screaming, each blaming the other for all that was going wrong in their lives. While it was apparent to Barbara that everyone in the family was in need of help, her husband fought the notion of any kind of counseling. Fortunately, Barbara eventually got help for herself and for her family. It's been a long and difficult journey, and they are still in the healing process; but hope and growth are coming into their marriage, their parenting and their personal lives.

Facet Thinking

Barbara's story graphically illustrates the confusing interconnected nature of human problems. Clearly, if one facet of life is unhealthy or out of balance, it affects all the others. Barbara's family was definitely what most counselors would call dysfunctional, but what was the root problem?

Was it primarily emotional? Mental? Volitional? Behavioral? Physical? Interpersonal? In the family system?

You've guessed it. The answer again is . . . "Yes!"

As Barbara or any of us moves toward the healthy balance discussed in the last chapter, all seven facets shown below are involved. Just as each facet of a diamond is inseparable from the diamond as a whole, the emotional, mental, volitional, behavioral, physical, interpersonal and familial aspects of our lives are also inseparable. This interconnectedness works to bring us both joy and pain, health and dysfunction.

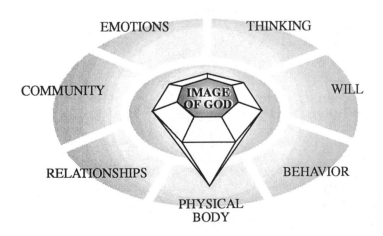

Genesis 1:27 tells us that God created us in His own image. We were created to reflect the *imago Dei*, the image of God, throughout every facet of our personhood. In the same way that a flawless diamond reflects light, we were designed to show the glory of our perfect and loving Creator in many different and beautiful ways.

I'm Dysfunctional, We're Dysfunctional

The diamond, then, is a good symbol for the wholeness that was our birthright as children of God — and before they fell into Sin, Adam and Eve reflected God's image brilliantly and without flaw through every facet. When Sin entered the world, however, all of the facets became distorted and blemished (dysfunctional). As a result, our human nature now reflects very little of the purity of God's image. In other words. . . because of Sin, our emotions are volatile, our minds are irrational, our wills are weakened, our behaviors are harmful, our bodies are diseased, our relationships are sinful and our family systems are unhealthy.

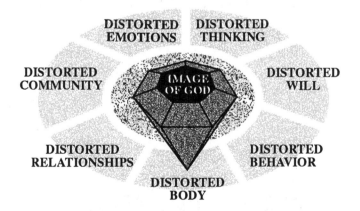

This is why God sent His Son, Jesus Christ, to earth. His plan was to restore our relationship with Himself and to bring a healthy balance back into our lives. Most Christians, of course, realize that knowing Christ doesn't instantaneously make us completely healthy or happy. But it *is* the first and most important step leading to complete restoration. If you have not taken this step and would like to, the following simple prayer has been provided to help you begin the process.

> *Lord Jesus, I ask You to come into my life. I trust You to take charge of my life and make me the kind of person You want me to be for this moment and forever. I confess my sins and I thank You for Your forgiveness and the assurance of eternal life in Your name. I expect now to receive the power of the Holy Spirit that I may share this faith, strength, joy and love with others in Jesus' name. Amen.*

If you have prayed this prayer or one like it, you have started a saving and *healing* relationship with Jesus Christ.

The Bible shows us that restoring all of the distorted facets of God's image is a joint venture between God and His children. We also know that growing toward health is a lifelong process, not a one-shot deal. It requires time, effort and our willing cooperation. This is the process that theologians refer to as *progressive sanctification*.

"But," you may ask, "wasn't all of that taken care of at the cross? Doesn't 2 Corinthians 5:17 tell us we are 'new creations' and that 'the old has gone, the new has come!' Why is this lifetime process necessary if that is true?" This is one of the most common questions I hear as a teacher and counselor. Unfortunately, the verse above is often quoted out of context, causing shame and confusion to many Christians like my friend Barbara who thought that Christian parents should have no family conflicts.

As believers, we live in a fallen world and continue to suffer from the distorting effects of Sin in the various facets of our lives even after taking the first step mentioned above. True, rebirth and restoration of our relationship with God is where the process of Christian growth begins; but it certainly doesn't stop there! When a child is born, the growth process begins in earnest. When a child of God is re-born, the same thing happens: there must be growth and growing pains.

That is what the Greek word *teleios* implies — a process of restoring completeness or wholeness to our lives. We can look forward with the Apostle Paul to the day when God, ". . .who began a good work in you, will carry it on to completion until the day of Jesus Christ" (Philippians 1:6).

What Ever Happened to Sin?

In the past several decades, it has become unpopular in many counseling circles to talk about Sin. This is unfortunate because one of the greatest obstacles to growth is misunderstanding or underestimating the destructive power that Sin has in our lives. When Sin and its various dimensions are misunderstood, God's antidote will be misapplied or missed altogether. The reason for analyzing Sin is to find its solutions rather than to encourage condemnation or hopelessness.

So what do we mean when we talk about Sin? And how does Sin influence our lives and relationships?

A complete and accurate definition is more difficult than you might imagine. There are several distinct Hebrew and Greek words translated as "Sin" in the Old and New Testaments and each conveys a slightly different idea. As I have studied their meanings and sought to understand what the Bible teaches us by using these words, I have come to realize that Sin has at least four major categories.

The first aspect of Sin is widely accepted. Most people agree that violating Scriptural laws such as the Ten Commandments constitutes sinning. This definition is compatible with The American Heritage Dictionary's definition of sin as *"a transgression of a religious or moral law, especially when deliberate."*[1] This intentional disobedience is what theologians call **rebellion.**

The second definition given in The American Heritage Dictionary touches on a less conspicuous aspect of Sin. It defines sin as *"a condition of estrangement from God as a result of breaking God's law."* According to Isaiah 59:2, when we rebel against God's laws, our **guilt** estranges or separates us from Him. In this case we're referring to true moral guilt.

It's important not to confuse guilt with *guilt feelings.* I've met people who have committed terrible crimes and don't *feel* guilty at all. Others, like my friend Barbara, experience anguished feelings over events for which they have had no moral responsibility.

Let me illustrate what I mean by true moral guilt. Recently, after a teaching trip, I was driving home on the interstate highway at midnight. I was in a hurry to get home and I let my speedometer creep up over the 55-mile-an-hour speed limit. Since there were no other cars on the highway, I didn't feel guilty about going ten miles an hour over the limit. But when the patrolman pulled me over and asked if I realized how fast I was going, I had to say, "Yes." Even though I didn't feel guilty (I was feeling angry), I *was* morally and legally guilty of breaking the law and had to pay the fine.

What Barbara was experiencing in the story I related earlier wasn't biblical guilt at all. It was **shame.** I have learned to make a strong distinction between the two. While guilt indicates that I deserve to suffer consequences (justice) for wrongful actions, shame reflects my *internal* judgment of my behavior and of my worth as a human being. Whether I'm truly guilty or not, shame involves the rejection of myself as a person and the condemnation of myself because of that.

Shame is like a distorted mirror that reflects only hideousness. Unlike honest remorse, shame operates like those trick mirrors you find in carnival fun houses. It exaggerates and distorts our flaws, faults and failures. It deceives us into believing we're inferior and less worthy of love than others or that, for some reason, we deserve to be humiliated or shunned. Shame is doubly insidious because it leads us to hide our true selves from others and cuts us off from receiving their help and love. The next chapter will focus further on how shame affects identity.

The fourth aspect of Sin is **bondage**. Persistent patterns of rebellion, guilt and shame accumulate over time to weaken and destroy our ability to initiate healthy change. We eventually become "stuck" in our sins and have difficulty even recognizing healthy choices. This spiritual, mental and emotional blindness contributes to addictions, compulsions, diseases and feelings of hopelessness.

Since we left Eden, every human being has been born into a world that is in bondage to Sin. We are influenced by generations of unresolved and unrecognized Sin in our social and family environments. Just as Barbara's daughter's behavior adversely influenced the rest of her family and gave birth to more problems and dysfunction, Sin's influence tends to multiply from generation to generation. Most of us begin absorbing unhealthy habits, attitudes, beliefs and relationship patterns even before we begin to walk and talk.

You can see how all four aspects of Sin combine to perpetuate a cycle of despair and dysfunction. They are also closely interrelated. Because I'm born into bondage, I have an innate tendency toward rebellion. When I rebel, my guilt estranges me from God. I feel ashamed and I hide. As Sin tightens its grip, I discover that I'm unable to initiate healthy change. In other words I'm caught in deeper bondage and the cycle continues.

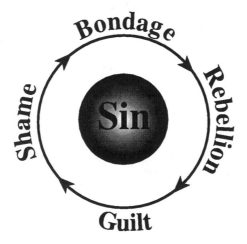

Everyone struggles with this cycle of Sin. The Apostle Paul tells us in Romans 7:14, 15:

> *We know that the law is spiritual; but I am unspiritual, sold as a slave to sin. I do not understand what I do. For what I want to do I do not do, but what I hate I do.*

Before we move on to embrace God's grace in Chapter 8 of the book of Romans, let's take a look at how Sin influences our lives and relationships. A complete and truthful picture of personhood or personality must include an understanding of how Sin affects our relationship with God, ourselves and others. Let's start with Adam and Eve.

A Biblical View of Personality

In the Garden, Adam and Eve were naked and unashamed (Genesis) and stood before the Father with nothing to hide. Their hearts were open to God and to each other. The graphic below illustrates how those early days in Eden must have been — a man and his wife who lived in loving intimacy with each other and had an open, intimate relationship with their Creator.

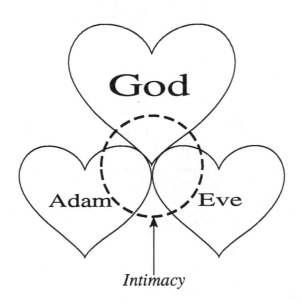

Intimacy

Then came the Fall, and as a result they became trapped in the malignant cycle of Sin. The most profound impact of the Fall has to do with what happened to the hearts of our ancestors. Although they had once been naked and unashamed, they now covered themselves, unable to escape the guilt and shame. The ensuing conversation between them and God revealed a deeper issue of the heart. When confronted by the Father about his disobedience, Adam blamed Eve; and she, finding no one else to accuse, blamed Satan for her own behavior.

These responses were the first expression of what counselors call defense mechanisms. Since then, all of us have inherited a tendency to deny the reality of our responsibility and enter into denial, blame shifting, suppression, etc. As Jeremiah 17:9 says, "the heart is deceitful above all things, and desperately wicked; who can know it?"

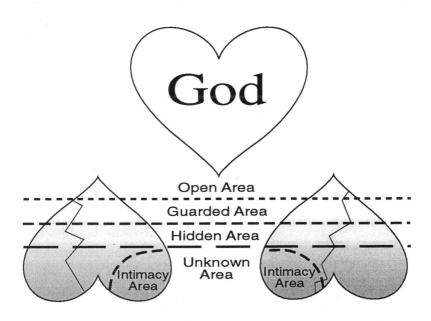

Now, following the Fall, the part of ourselves we're willing to share with God and others is like the tip of an iceberg.

Underneath the surface, protected by a formidable array of defenses, are the memories, thoughts, experiences and beliefs that we hide in shame. Still farther down, below the level of conscious awareness, lies the deep heart. Originally created for intimacy with God and others, this part of us is the most heavily defended. The secret hurts, repressed memories and desires that we can't or won't face are accumulated here in complete darkness. Unresolved traumas and toxic beliefs combine with the pollution of hidden Sin to distort our outlook and keep us in bondage. But God provides us with a plan for finding release and healing.

Applying Grace

So, how can we escape from this awful bondage and find freedom for ourselves so we can help others? The answer is clear. We must learn to *apply grace*. Grace is the unmerited favor and mercy God extends to all of His Children. John 1:17 tells us that "grace and truth came through Jesus Christ." But what does this mean? The New Testament Greek word for grace is *charis*. Our modern words charisma and charismatic are derived from it. The idea expressed is of a wonderful gift, undeserved, but freely given.

Individually, we must open our hearts to receive God's grace: His wonderful gifts of caring love, acceptance and worth. As Christians, we can help one another receive and apply God's grace by growing and using the fruit of the Spirit in our daily relationships. As we demonstrate God's love and grace to others through warm, empathic listening and deep respect, we can help them gently uncover powerful feelings that have gotten stuck deep within their hearts:

- Feelings of shame and rejection.
- Memories of betrayal and abuse.
- Secret longings and unfulfilled desires.
- Memories of cheating, lying or harming others.
- Rational and irrational fears.
- Painful or embarrassing secrets.

Even in the face of God's love, most of us intuitively defend the sanctuary of our deepest thoughts and feelings through:

- Denial
- Joking
- Withdrawing
- Attacking
- Workaholism
- Rationalizing
- Controlling
- Perfectionism
- Spiritualizing

I think of the heart as a well-defended fortress, constructed to keep out anyone or anything that might present a threat. Even well-meaning friends and family members may be defeated in their helping attempts by a daunting array of automatic defense strategies. At the first sign of threat, the doors of the deep heart slam, closing helpers out and leaving us alone again with our pain.

I recently received a poem from one of our seminar leaders. It captures an attitude of tender compassion and powerfully states the reasons for extending grace to ourselves and others.

I've been unable to identify the author, but I'd like to share it with you:

> *i will present you*
> *parts*
> *of*
> *my*
> *self*
> *slowly*
> *if you are patient and tender.*
> *i will open drawers*
> *that mostly stay closed*
> *and bring out places and people and things*
> *sounds and smells, loves and frustrations, hopes and sadnesses,*
> *bits and pieces of three decades of life*
> *that have been grabbed off*
> *in chunks*
> *and found lying in my hands.*
> *they have eaten*
> *their way into*
> *my heart.*
> *altogether - you or i will never see them -*

they are me.
if you regard them lightly,
deny that they are important
or worse, judge them
i will quietly, slowly,
begin to wrap them up,
in small pieces of velvet,
like worn silver and gold jewelry,
tuck them away
in a small wooden chest of drawers

and close.

You can see that tenderness and patience are essential when we deal with issues of the sensitive areas of the heart.

Sadly, many well-intentioned people assume that the best way to help others is to simply confront their sinful behavior. Certainly, accurate confrontation is an essential part of growth; but it will activate our defense mechanisms unless a caring relationship has first been established to support the pain of accountability.

I've had many personal experiences with the need to build a bridge of care and confidence before sharing my "incredible wisdom" or insights. Most of my own failures as a helper can be traced to impatience and a desire to straighten folks out.

In most situations, pursuing immediate change through confrontation and denunciation of Sin meets with stunning failure. Galatians 6:1 says, "If someone is caught in a sin, you who are spiritual should restore him gently." Rather than acting confrontationally, it's far more helpful to employ the Spirit's fruit of *love, joy, peace, patience, kindness, goodness, faithfulness, gentleness and self-control* (Galatians 5:22, 23). In this way, we extend grace so that people can sense our care and respect, attributes most likely to encourage people to open up the hidden aspects of their hearts.

Think about it. To whom would you confide a sensitive personal issue? I wasn't feeling well one day at church and spoke that fact openly to a friend's question of "How are you?" Her reply was a tense and somewhat parental "Don't say that! You're giving a negative confession!" Not only did she have poor theology, she had bad manners and awful helping skills.

Even if my friend's advice had been accurate, the timing and tone were all wrong. It's God's love, not His wrath, that calls us to repentance. Similarly, it's the love and grace of others that give me the strength to examine the secret places of my heart. Patience and caring love help me overcome my ever-present sense of shame and self-condemnation.

If we continue to hide behind fig leaves of denial, defensiveness and secrecy, we can't experience the freedom of walking in the light. Fig leaves fester and multiply in the damp darkness of the deep-heart dungeon. The fear of others' rejection and God's condemnation encourages the same cover-ups that Adam and Eve modeled. Speaking the Gospel (good news) to hurting friends and colleagues stands as a beacon of hope and love in the midst of the world's bad news. The Gospel calls us to love people just as they are to give them the courage to "walk in the light as He is in the light" (1 John 1:7a). Walking in the light produces fellowship, harmony and intimacy with one another and with God (1 John 1:5-7).

Through the cross of Christ, we have a remedy for the problem of Sin. The Circle of Grace summarizes the application of grace to all four aspects of Sin. This applies to all people. For our **rebellion**, God provides us with a free invitation to return to Him as did the wayward son in Luke 15:17-20. For our **guilt**, God offers complete forgiveness when we confess and restore a clean relationship with Him (1 John 1:8, 9). For our **shame**, God provides us with His truth to renew our thinking (Romans 12:2). Finally, for our **bondage,** He provides His power to help us overcome the world, the flesh and the devil (2 Corinthians 10:3-5).

For a more thorough discussion of Sin and Grace, let me refer you to my *Theology of a Caring, Equipping Community.* [2]

If all of this talk of Sin and Grace is too theological or a little bit confusing to you, the important idea to remember is that it is by caring, nonjudgmental relationships that we communicate God's love and grace to others. When we do, the deep heart can more readily open up to the light. Walking in grace-filled fellowship encourages, supports and rewards fellowship with God, self and others. And what are the greatest commandments?

Love God, and *love your neighbor as yourself*!

Our next Chapter will show how we can discover the basis for developing a healthy identity and accurate self-esteem.

Identity: More Than a Reflection

There's a wonderful children's book by P.D. Eastman called *Are You My Mother?*[1]

The story is about a baby bird who hatches while his mother is away from the nest. Immediately, the bird begins searching for his absent mother. Not knowing what she looks like, he goes right by her. Seeking high and low, he asks all of the animals in the barnyard if they are his mother. He even asks a boat and an airplane, but to no avail. Throughout the book, he is deeply discouraged and afraid until he finally finds his mother. After that, he is confident and happy because he knows who he is.

This simple children's story contains a profound parable about human nature. It points to the fact that something in each of us longs not only to discover *who* we are but *whose* we are. On the natural level, it's important to know we belong.

God's Likeness: More Than Reflection

On the spiritual level, like the baby bird, we've searched for the answers to the mystery of our existence in some pretty unusual places. Without realizing it, many of us have passed by the only reliable foundation for building a healthy identity or self-image — a true understanding of our relationship to God. The first step in discovering the truth about ourselves is found in Genesis 1:27, which states that men and women are unique in all of the universe because we are made in God's "own image." We alone bear His "likeness" or family resemblance.

This is the very bedrock of healthy identity and self-esteem. It's what sets us apart from all creation and every other creature on the planet.

A beautiful work of art or a great book reflects its creator. In the same way, Scripture tells us we have been intentionally designed in God's image. Human beings are not just an evolutionary coincidence, as some would have us believe; we are God's self portraits!

But what does that mean?

Consider some of the ways that we resemble our Maker. The Heavenly Father made us self-aware. He gave us a capacity for independent thought and action as well as the ability to perceive and interpret complex information. He gave us the gifts of intellect and imagination, the ability to make tools and to create fine works of art, literature and science.

We are distinct individuals; but regardless of the nationality or culture we are born into, we share in God's desire for communication and connection with persons other than ourselves. We've been given the ability to exercise free will, make plans, anticipate results and make major choices that affect our destinies. We can choose to use these capacities as God directs or we can misuse, neglect or ignore what He has given us.

Unlike the fish, the birds, and other animals mentioned in Genesis, we alone have the capacity for a dynamic relationship with our Maker.

The importance of *persons* is shown in the order of creation in Chapter 1 of Genesis. God began by making the heavens and the earth, forming the sun, the seas, the fish, the fowl, the beasts of the field and everything that grows. In each case, He pronounced these creations "good."

34

But there was still something missing. Those creatures of the air and the sea and the land could not share or relate to God's thoughts and feelings. In other words, they lacked *personality*. God then chose to create humankind in His likeness — with the power to share intimately in His thoughts and feelings, in His friendship and love.

After making the first man and woman, God's evaluation of His work wasn't just another "it was good" like before. After making Adam and Eve in His own image, God looked at them and said that "it was *very* good" (Genesis 1:31). This powerful appraisal of human worth continues to resound to us today, even in the midst of our confusion and shame.

Tadpoles or Angels: Unraveling the Mystery

Once we accept a Scriptural basis for identity and self-worth, it becomes a guide to help us to better understand and appreciate the love God has for *all* people. A love that found its fullest expression at the cross.

Thomas Carlyle, the famous English author, once addressed a meeting of scholars concerning the meaning of persons. "Gentlemen," he said, "you place man a little higher than the tadpole. I hold with the ancient singer, 'thou hast made him a little lower than the angels.' "

Carlyle was referring to David's pronouncement of human worth from the Psalms:

> *For thou hast made him a little lower than the angels, and hast crowned him with glory and honour. Thou madest him to have dominion over the works of thy hands; thou hast put all things under his feet.* (Psalm 8:5,6 KJV)

It's ironic that the 1611 King James version of the Bible quoted by Carlyle actually understates the intention of the Hebrew text of Psalm 8. The word translated as "angels" is *'elohiym*, used more than 2300 times in the Old Testament to refer to God. Most modern translations correctly render the passage,

"You have made him a little lower than God." We can only speculate why the 1611 translators couldn't bring themselves to accept the potent implications of an accurate translation. Perhaps they, like many Christians, just couldn't let go of their shame and accept God's view of persons.

Still with this declaration, the respected Carlyle zeroed in on the central question of human identity. Either we are an advanced animal form — the most advanced to date, as the product of some random accident of evolution — or we are children of a living and loving God. Our entire identity, in fact, hinges on this very issue.

By making us in His image, God identified us directly with Himself and clearly emphasized His estimation of our intrinsic value. We may not completely understand it; but if we accept the view that we are God's image bearers, we must also accept His astonishingly high assessment of our personal worth. I esteem myself because I esteem God. Low self-esteem actually implies a low opinion of God.

Sadly, it's often Christians who most grossly undervalue human worth, believing it is somehow more spiritual to devalue and despise themselves than it is to accept God's truth. Self-hatred and poor self-esteem may masquerade as humility; but in reality they often result from stubborn disobedience, a low opinion of God or a complete misunderstanding of the Scriptures. True humility and obedience rest in accepting God's opinion of *who* we are and *whose* we are, even if it goes against our shame-based cultural or religious beliefs.

But, you ask, what about Sin? To answer this frequently asked question, I'll tell you about Dean, a jeweler friend.

Dean once told me how he found a hidden treasure at an estate sale. Sorting through dusty old boxes of cheap costume jewelry, his professional eye spotted a particular piece. In an inferior sterling silver setting, covered with decades of accumulated grime and dullness, was a large black opal. No doubt, you and I would have overlooked it, dismissing it as junk. But with his trained eye, he knew it was worth several thousand dollars and that skillful polishing and a new setting would eventually reveal the beauty hidden beneath the dust and dirt.

Just as Dean's skillful eye perceived hidden value amidst shabby and mediocre trinkets, God looks through the tarnish and pollution of Sin to see His blurred image hidden inside us. Our value doesn't come from our *works* but from our built-in *worth*. It doesn't come from anything we do or believe; it comes from God's image within us.

Many wonder how we can focus on positive self-worth when the world is filled with the ugliness of Sin. Weren't we all ruined when Adam and Eve sinned? Doesn't their disobedience render us basically worthless? Absolutely not!

The New Testament writers clearly recognized and valued the image of God even in fallen human beings. James warns against condemning or cursing people, "who have been made in God's likeness" (James 3:9). And in spite of all the sins and failures of the Christians at Corinth, Paul told them they were "the image and glory of God" (1 Corinthians 11:7).

Naturally, Sin corrupts our lives and distorts the image of God within us, but by no means destroys it completely. God dramatically confirmed His estimate of our worth by sending Jesus to the cross for us. When Jesus counted the cost in Gethsemane before going to Golgotha, He affirmed that sinful humanity was worth the sacrifice of His life.

He decided that we were worth it. *I am worth it* and *you are worth it!*

No matter how dramatically things have changed during the centuries since the Fall, this basic truth and basis for true self-worth has remained constant. No matter what your present state in life, no matter what your past transgressions and failings, no matter what your innermost thoughts and feelings, God loves you. Because He made you in His image, He wants to restore you to wholeness.

Romans 5:8 tells us that "while we were still sinners, Christ died for us." Christ came to save us from the power of Sin. His death was designed to restore us to wholeness in our relationships with God, self and others. This sets the stage for us as caring helpers because our goals are the same: restored relationships.

Self-esteem Redeemed

There's no doubt that self-esteem is deeply damaged by the power of Sin and by our individual acts of disobedience or sins. Throughout the history of Christianity the question of whether our self-esteem can truly be restored has been a controversial point. My answer to this question is a resounding "Yes!"

As we know, Scripture commands us to love our neighbors as we love ourselves. Unfortunately, that's what many of us do — but not in the way God intended. Some of us despise ourselves and our neighbors equally! Most of us love our neighbors about as well as we love ourselves — which isn't very much.

What a shame!

Think about it. If you detest yourself, it's difficult to truly love anyone else. Years of study and counseling experience have convinced me that a healthy self-image and balanced self-esteem are vital components of spiritual health. As one Bible teacher said, "You have to *have* a self before you can give your self away."

This doesn't mean I'm completely comfortable with the pop psychology connected with what has come to be called the Self-esteem Movement. Much of it is flawed and some of it is just plain ridiculous.

During the last few decades, just about every segment of western society — from education to business and industry — has jumped on the self-esteem bandwagon. It started in the 1970s with such best sellers as *I'm OK, You're OK*[2] and *Pulling Your Own Strings*.[3] Since then, self-esteem has been proclaimed the long-awaited solution to every problem under the sun.

People looking for a magic elixir to cure everything from anxiety and depression to drug abuse and teen pregnancy have rallied under the banner of self-esteem. Like many other Christians, I find the current "gospel of self-esteem" theologically and psychologically lacking. In addition, it often has the opposite effect from what its proponents intend.

In the early '70s, I worked with Barney Ford, the director of Intervarsity Christian Fellowship at the University of Cincinnati. As a former math and computer major, he had a marvelous way of cutting to the bottom line on issues of philosophy and theology. Barney would say, "When anyone asks me what $2 + 2$ is, I always ask them another question: 'What base number system are you using?' " A base number system of three gives a different answer than if the base is ten.

Healthy self-esteem depends on some basic assumptions as well. When discussing self-esteem and its detractors, a couple of definitions are in order. Let's start with what self-esteem isn't. The opposite of a positive self-image is *shame*, which has to do with the loss of identity and inheritance that every person experiences because of Sin. Whereas guilt points to the fact (not the feeling) of separation from God and others, shame points to the theological and psychological *fact* of lost identity/inheritance. The Hebrew word for shame, *bwash*, reinforces this idea. It means "drained of life" or "pale of face," terms which describe the human response to our lost condition. We have "lost face" with God, others and ourselves.

There are shame-based families and shame-based cultures. For many of us, any failure to be perfect leads to loss of face and perhaps total rejection. A pilot from a shame-based Asian country recently committed suicide because he landed improperly and believed he had lost face with the whole country.

The messages and beliefs we internalize deeply influence our self-image and how we feel. Think about how you would describe yourself apart from your credentials, job, family, political views, hobbies, religion or goals. Who are you apart from what you do? What situations trigger your feelings? Look at the list below and fill in situations that elicit unpleasant emotions in you.

- I feel lonely when. . .
- I feel afraid when. . .
- I feel ashamed when. . .
- I feel sad when. . .
- I feel angry when. . .
- I feel discouraged when. . .
- I feel nervous when. . .

Your feelings and beliefs are probably tied to memories of how others have responded to you. We are all surrounded by expectations, evaluations, and judgements. Some are spoken, but many are silent or hidden. They are modeled by parents, siblings, peers and authority figures and influence how we respond to life and how we see ourselves.

Think about how the important people in your life have influenced you. Most of the messages you have internalized about your worth and value probably come from others either directly or indirectly. When you feel condemned, defeated, rejected, ashamed or worthless, who do you hear speaking?

For some, it might be the voice of:

- an angry parent
- an unkind teacher
- a critical coach
- a playground bully
- a perfectionistic boss

Whoever it is for you, it's important to remember that accurate self-esteem can only be based on discovering our true identity and our eternal inheritance, and then standing on that truth regardless of circumstances.

The Prince and the Pauper

The reason that classic children's stories and fairy tales are so popular in every society is, I believe, because they speak universally to the human conditions of guilt, shame, redemption and forgiveness – issues that every human being faces, regardless of culture. Many of these classic accounts have to do with how humans feel about themselves. One tale illustrates our search for identity and significance in an especially powerful way. In *The Prince and the Pauper*, we find two boys who "traded places," and yet each carries his pre-exchange belief about himself into his new situation.

Although the destitute pauper receives beautiful new clothes, a powerful new title, lush new surroundings and a full kingly inheritance, he steadfastly views himself as a helpless, weak, poverty-stricken child who will never amount to anything. He is convinced that he will lose everything if he makes any mistakes and is overwhelmed with anxiety, fear and self-condemnation.

This sounds an awful lot like many Christians that I know.

I can think of no more powerful parable for what happens when God reaches down and redeems one of His guilty, shame-filled creatures. The guilt is removed and intimacy is restored with our Creator. And, more powerful still to our sense of self-worth and our self-esteem, we are adopted as sons into the Father's forever-family!

Adoption is possibly the most neglected topic in the church. Just go to a bookstore and count the number of books written on guilt and forgiveness. There are quite a few. Many, in fact, wrongly conclude that our search for a significant self-image is to be found in forgiveness. While crucial to mental, emotional, spiritual and physical health, this is *not* the answer to low self-esteem.

While rarely emphasized, adoption forms the foundation for a healthy biblical self-respect, both theologically and psychologically. When we're afraid we're not good enough or that we don't measure up, we can turn to Romans 8:15 (KJV), which states: "For you did not receive the spirit of bondage again to fear, but you received the Spirit of adoption by whom we cry out, 'Abba, Father.' " Through Christ's sacrifice, we have been adopted into God's family. The Aramaic word *Abba* expresses the heart of tenderness and intimacy in our relationship with God. In English the closest translation would be *daddy* or *papa*. It was a term reserved only for children; slaves were forbidden to use it.

Like shame, adoption is a relational term. In place of our self-rejection, God provides acceptance and assurance of being loved. In his classic book *Knowing God*, J. I. Packer discusses what it means to be adopted and to have God as our Father:

> *Our maker becomes our perfect parent faithful in love and care, generous and thoughtful, interested in all we do, respecting our individuality, skillful in training us, wise in guidance, always available, helping us to find ourselves in maturity, integrity, and uprightness is a thought which can have meaning for everybody, whether we come to it saying, "I had a wonderful father and I see that God is like that, only more so," or by saying, "My father disappointed me here, and here, and here, but God, praise his name, will be very different," or even by saying, "I have never known what it is to have a father on earth, but thank God I now have one in heaven."* [4]

The fact of adoption and the work of Christ on the cross eliminate our theological shame for eternity. Along with the biblical truth of the *Imago Dei*, adoption provides us with a basis for dealing with the psychological scars of fear, anxiety, hiding and self-hatred left by shame. At a recent workshop, a pastor asked me to talk about healthy shame. I had to reply, "There is no such animal!"

There's no way that shame can be good. To confuse shame with embarrassment is similar to confusing guilt with anxiety. Both lose their biblical meaning and, thus, their redemptive character. Reducing true moral guilt to "guilt feelings" and shame to "embarrassed feelings" is to rob the cross of its power and its ability to restore our minds to peace and sanity.

When we are adopted into the family of God, we gain an indestructible new identity. A new spirit and new title and new eternity are ours. By receiving this new title as a "son of God" (Galatians 4:4-7), every Christian becomes an heir of God and a co-heir with Christ.

Since many of us have not grasped these radical truths about identity and inheritance, we, like the pauper, fail to live as "children of the Heavenly Father." We continue to insist to ourselves and to others that we don't deserve this new designation. So we go through life denying what Jesus paid so dearly to buy for us. But renewing our minds with the truth about our self-worth can lead to peace and power. One of the reasons our course *Rational Christian Thinking*[5] is so helpful is that it promotes a tool for reinforcing these truths.

The only lasting antidote for shame and its emotional consequences of low self-esteem, insecurity, fear and self-condemnation is grasping the truth of adoption. We must hang on to it for dear life — even in opposition to our pauper-conditioned thoughts and feelings.

To attempt to raise the self-esteem of another person without these truths is not only futile, but disrespectful. Some say, "Yes, you are an accident of history that is equal in worth to a bug, but you are *great!*" Evolutionary teaching is one common cause for low self-esteem in this country, followed closely by misguided Christians who teach that it's godly to demean ourselves.

By the way, as a therapist who deals often with these issues, I sometimes find women who misunderstand the term, "sons of God," and who feel further loss of self-respect. This term is used in the Scripture because in those days the eldest son inherited the father's wealth. In other words, we're being informed that every child of God, regardless of gender or sibling placement, is an eldest son with a *full* inheritance from the Father. So, ladies, you are a first born son of the Heavenly Father in terms of spiritual inheritance.

Now a final word to those who struggle with constant feelings of "guilt and shame." If you've been emotionally, sexually or physically abused, you may need therapy from a wise counselor to help you assimilate the truths I talked about above. At our hospital and counseling centers, this is one of the most prevalent issues with which we deal. You can find hope for healing, but be patient and remember the process takes time. In the book *Rational Christian Thinking*[6], we describe a process for renewing the mind that offers powerful healing for wounded hearts and minds. One of the authors of that course, Dr. Alice Petersen, offers this reminder to herself and all who struggle with shame and poor self-esteem, "What God says about me is more important than what the whole world says!"

Here are some Scriptures that point to who you are if you know Christ. I find these personally helpful in renewing my thinking about who I am in Christ.

I am forgiven.. Ephesians 1:7
I am a new creation.............................2 Corinthians 5:17
I am loved.. Jeremiah 31:3
I am alive with Christ................................Ephesians 2:5
I am more than a conqueror..........................Romans 8:37
I am a co-heir with Christ.............................Romans 8:17
I am free from condemnation.........................Romans 8:1
I am hopeful...Colossians 1:27
I am moving towards wholeness.................Philippians 1:6
I have everlasting life.....................................John 6:47

Now let's turn to some practical suggestions that will help us recognize and overcome communication barriers that separate us from God and other people.

The Fax About Communication

Engineer and inventor Charles F. Kettering once complained, "We can communicate an idea around the world in seventy seconds, but it sometimes takes years for an idea to get through 1/4 inch of human skull."

Communications technology has advanced considerably since Mr. Kettering's day. I regularly fax letters all over the world from my office in Cincinnati. In less than 14 seconds my letters can travel the 4,960 miles to a friend in Moscow or perhaps traverse 9,370 miles to a pastor in Sydney.

Sending a fax is simple once you understand how the basic process works. I dial a fax number, my machine scans the letter I'm sending with its sensors and then codes its visible image into a series of beeping sounds and electrical impulses.

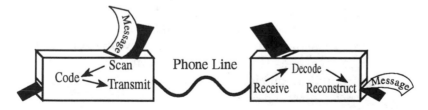

My machine then transmits those sounds across the phone lines to another fax machine that receives them, decodes them and reconstructs a facsimile of the original letter. If there's no interference or distortion on the phone line, the receiving machine will signal my machine that the letter has been received and printed out.

When we as human beings communicate, we follow steps similar to my fax machine — only we're considerably more complex and much faster. We scan our memories, mental and emotional perceptions, abstract ideas and all of our five senses for the message we want to communicate. Then, at unimaginable speeds, we transform or code our message into words, symbols, pictures and/or non-verbal gestures that we can transmit to another person. With the amazing gift of language, we're able to send messages of incredible subtlety and complexity. . . messages colored and flavored by our unique culture, experiences and beliefs.

We can receive the messages another person sends and attempt to decode them by filtering their symbols through our own unique set of experiences, perceptions, prejudices and beliefs. If we're not careful, this is the point where common communication barriers can interfere with our ability to accurately receive, interpret and reconstruct the messages that were sent.

Unlike a simple fax machine, you and I have the capacity to send and receive several levels of communication simultaneously. Part of the difficulty we have in accurately decoding and reconstructing the messages we send is that in any communication there are at least six separate messages :

1. The message I intend to convey.
2. The message I verbalize.
3. The message my body language sends.
4. The message you actually hear.
5. The message you understand from what you hear.
6. The messages that are triggered in your personal memories and emotions .

Because these various types of messages all interact with one another in different ways, sorting through them to find accurate and clear communication can be a real challenge. In terms of human interaction, the complexity of decoding, reconstructing and sorting out all of these messages accurately is often difficult and makes communication problems and misunderstandings inevitable.

A fax machine trying to send and receive six separate messages at once would probably produce a scrambled mess! But we can do it.

Unlike a fax machine, we can improve our communication by addressing several key barriers that distort our understanding and lead to unnecessary conflict and confusion. These barriers to effective communication tend to fall into three categories: *problems of focus, problems of feeling* and *problems of fellowship*.

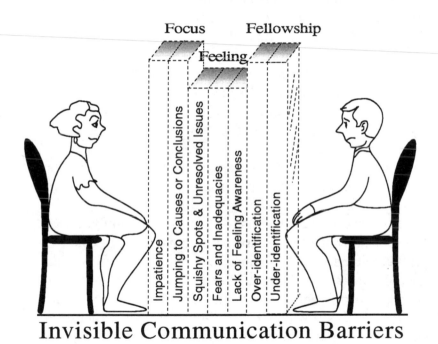

Invisible Communication Barriers

Focus Problems

Did you know that our minds generate words at least five times faster than we can verbalize them? Or that we can absorb six pages of typed words in less than one-third the time it takes to read them aloud?

It's hard to imagine that our brain's speed and efficiency could operate to actually obstruct communication — but that's just what it does. Our gray matter works so fast that we have to slow it down considerably before we can listen effectively to others. This requires energy and focus.

Have you ever been listening intently to someone only to suddenly realize that you've momentarily "tuned them out"? Your mind, instead of tracking with what's being said, is off on a journey of its own! That's what I'm talking about when I say that effective communication requires focused energy. As a professional counselor I use listening as an important tool in my job, but I must admit that my mind sometimes wanders when others are talking.

In fact, now and then my thoughts wander ahead of what people are saying. I'm too busy thinking of what I'm going to say next. At other times I become so intrigued with an interesting concept someone has expressed that I'm busily examining it while that person moves on with the conversation. Then there are those times when I'm so preoccupied with my own thoughts and feelings that I don't give others my complete attention.

As a Christian who desires to show compassion and caring, I have to consciously work at "staying with" the people who are talking to me. I have to rein in my mind's natural tendency to wander ahead or behind what's actually being said. For me, disciplining myself to slow down and listen to others at their own pace has proven to be a key to deeper understanding, deeper compassion and increased helpfulness.

Impatience

Cultivating an understanding heart requires patience. First Thessalonians 5:14 tells us to "be patient with everyone." But my crowded work and family schedules seem to dictate the opposite attitude. Many of us have fallen prey to the frantic pace of modern living. Perhaps we've even begun to resent the "interruptions" brought on by personal relationships. We may find listening to friends while they sort through their thoughts and feelings laborious and painfully time-consuming. So we fidget impatiently, hoping they will "get to the point" or "get on with it."

I remember speaking to a group several years ago on the importance of demonstrating the fruit of the Spirit by listening patiently to others. A woman in the audience aptly expressed what many of us secretly wonder. "Showing the fruit of the Spirit sounds like a good idea, Gary," she said, "but when do we get to *sock it to 'em* time?"

Such impatience may result from a conscious belief that somehow I should have "the right answer" to everyone's problems. If they would just be quiet long enough for me to tell them what to do, everything would be fine. If I adopt this kind of attitude, I feel intense pressure to provide quick answers or instant solutions to their problems, no matter how long-standing or complex the problems may be.

While this approach may be taken with all good intentions to help another, in reality such a hurried, impatient attitude usually conveys just the opposite of Christian caring. If you've ever received this kind of "hasty helping," you know how condescending and disrespectful it can feel.

Jumping to causes and conclusions

Jumping to hasty conclusions or assuming that we have insight into the hidden causes of other people's actions is another common barrier to healthy communication.

A pastor friend of mine tells this story to illustrate the issue. While motoring down a winding mountain road, a driver spots a red convertible recklessly careening around the curve toward him. Honking and gesturing wildly as he flies past, the convertible's driver shouts, "PIG!" in a loud voice. In startled anger, my friend turns his head and yells back at the receding sports car, "YOU JERK!" Imagine his surprise, however, when he suddenly comes upon a huge hog that has wandered out into the road.

In much the same way that a movie projector works, we project our conclusions, assumptions and expectations on others and use them as a screen to reflect our own inner issues. This unhealthy process takes two forms:

- Jumping to cause — "You said that because you don't like women."

- Jumping to conclusions —"You're going to mess up your life if you don't go to school this fall!"

Besides the obvious drawback of often being wrong, jumping to causes also leads to broken relationships and poor communication. The same thing is true, of course, when we take a giant leap to a hastily drawn conclusion without taking time to listen fully to the person. Like the radio commentator Paul Harvey, we need to hear "the rest of the story."

Feeling Problems

In addition to "jumping," there are other reactions that can keep us from establishing effective communication patterns.

Squishy Spots and Unresolved Issues

A small group leader named Dale was listening to a man who had been abused by an alcoholic father. The man was relating how awful it was for him as a child to hear the sound of his dad pouring a drink because he knew it meant that physical abuse was almost certain to follow. At the moment Dale heard the phrase "the sound of my father pouring a drink," it was like a trigger; and his mind was suddenly transported back to his own painful childhood. Immersed in the ache of his own memories, Dale was unable to listen to any more of the story.

The speaker had unwittingly touched a "squishy spot" in Dale. Squishy spots are unresolved sensitive or painful personal issues that come up out of the deep heart and act as communication barriers. When those painful memories were triggered, Dale's concentration and ability to listen were blocked and his ability to be an effective helper was hindered.

Let's face it; even those of us who were raised in healthy, caring families have some upsetting memories. Familiar phrases, gestures or certain topics of conversation that we subconsciously associate with past events can trigger unpleasant memories or emotions. While I was in a Norwegian worship service several years ago, a certain song transported me backward into some very painful squishy spots. Although my family was no more dysfunctional than most, I had internalized several childhood traumas relating to my belief that Mother loved my elder brother more than me. That hidden and bitter memory was hindering me from working effectively with some people. Thankfully, the Lord began healing that hurt on a mountain in the center of Norway, and I'm no longer suffering from its effects.

Once they *are* triggered, squishy spots make it difficult for us to distinguish our feeling responses from what people are actually saying to us. Have you ever surprised yourself by reacting with unexpected anger, sadness or irritation to an off-handed comment? If so, the chances are that you were experiencing what happens when a squishy spot is touched.

Dealing effectively with our squishy spots requires emotional self-awareness and inner healing. If we're unaware of our feelings, they become an invisible obstacle to relating. It's important that we take our feelings seriously — no matter how trivial or unimportant they may seem at the time. Unless we are willing to face and work through the cause of unruly feelings, unresolved issues from the past can pollute current relationships and block our ability to help others.

Fears and Feelings of Inadequacy

Another kind of feeling problem is a chronic expectation of failure or inadequacy (shame).

Rita is a good example. Attending one of our seminars, this extremely quiet lady made an immediate impression on me. I eventually learned that Rita came from a painful family background. Later, she confided in me that she was surprised that she had enjoyed herself so much during the workshop.

"I've always felt so ashamed of myself and my family," she explained. "I never believed that there was anything I could do to help myself, let alone anybody else. This class taught me that I have something good to give, and it's O.K. to be a *wounded healer*."

Like many people, Rita was afraid she wasn't good enough to receive God's love or to give it away. She thought that only people who had conquered all their problems had anything to offer. In the past, her fears kept her from seeking help because she was too afraid to put into words the feelings that were crushing her spirit.

For Rita and many others like her, the genuine caring of another *wounded healer* made all of the difference in the world. Other wounded healers in her small group listened to her, respected her and accepted her just as she was. Since her first seminar a few years ago, I've watched Rita blossom. She has developed great confidence in God's ability to bring wholeness to her life and the lives of others. With God's help and with the support of caring, understanding helpers, she is overcoming her fearfulness and feelings of inadequacy.

Lack of Feeling Awareness

We are all like Rita to some degree because so much of our inner life is a mystery — even to ourselves.

As Jesus said, "Out of the overflow of the heart the mouth speaks" (Matthew 12:34); and that which comes out is not always pretty. I can't count the number of times my wife, Karen, has pointed out that I seemed angry, upset or depressed because of something in my voice or manner. In fact, she's often a better judge of my inner state than I am.

Like many men, I sometimes have difficulty getting in touch with my feelings. This can often be a significant barrier to communication because my inner life influences how I interpret what others say. The inner healing I experienced in Norway opened me up to a richer awareness of both the painful and the positive ways I experienced my childhood.

As long as I denied the reality of those feelings, they subtly but mysteriously affected my adult relationships. But once I faced them and felt them fully, I was able to connect more deeply with my family and those I counseled. God's ways are still the best. By staying in touch with my self, I improve my connections with others. Had I stayed in denial of those hurts and feelings, I might still be struggling with their influences.

Fellowship Problems

Sometimes the primary barrier to helping is not focus or feeling problems, but comes from relational or fellowship difficulties. Fellowship-oriented problems usually occur when we either over-identify or under-identify with another person. Over-identification is often called codependency, and under-identification is considered callousness.

Over-identification

Beth, for example, is a friend who gets very deeply involved with people, even in the movies. When she went to see *Jaws*, she got so involved that during the shark attack, she actually screamed and jumped into the lap of a stranger sitting next to her! It's for people like Beth that movies are made.

Logically, she knew these people on the screen were fictional characters and the situations weren't real. But emotionally, the events (presented in living color and with wrap-around sound) hit home and led her to over-identify with the characters and their feelings. And wow, was it a success, even if it was a little embarrassing!

Certainly, being able to relate to another's situation can be both admirable and helpful. But over-involvement gets us in trouble. In fact, we can feel completely overwhelmed by the problems of others — leading us to either withdraw from the relationship or, like Beth, get too involved. Over-identification can cause us to be terribly uncomfortable when we're attempting to help people who are experiencing deep emotions because we just can't separate our feelings from those of the people we're helping.

Can you remember a time when you began to have a deeply emotional experience only to be told by a "helper" to "stay calm" or "don't cry" or "now, now, it will all be O.K."? The "helper" probably identified with your feelings so much that he was unable to handle his own level of emotions.

These are natural human reactions and certainly nothing to hide, but growth into healthy Helpers requires us to overcome these various barriers. In fact, potential helpers who think they're immune to these temptations are being unrealistic. Even professionally trained therapists must be willing to grow.

Under-identification

When it comes to unbalanced compassion responses, we can also tip the scales in the direction of not caring enough. Differences such as gender, cultural background, education, personal experiences and even genetics can cause us to perceive the world differently from others. When two or more persons from diverse backgrounds try to communicate, they often find that accuracy and real understanding are difficult because they simply can't relate to what the other person is talking about.

The Aborigines, for example, are a tribe of hunters and gatherers who are unjustifiably regarded by some Australians as being lazy. In actuality, nothing could be further from the truth. The Aborigines often spend six- to eight-hour stretches of time out in the bush, picking tiny berries for their nourishment. It's not at all unusual for them to spend all day hunting and gathering in order to get a single day's supply of food. But the cultural and economic differences between the Aborigines and the Europeans are so great that misunderstanding and conflict are almost guaranteed.

Although this is an extreme example, certainly you've found yourself in situations where you simply cannot connect with another person's problem. So you can relate to Mr. Kettering's observation about how difficult it is to communicate through a quarter-inch of the human skull. In fact, the greatest barriers are sometimes found in our own homes and churches where one would think that understanding would be the easiest.

When Karen and I first married, it was my habit to spontaneously invite friends over for a meal or a board game. What I didn't realize about our relationship was the fact that we were very different in many ways. In the first place, I was not concerned about how neat or messy the house looked. Karen was! Second, I was an extrovert who *gained* energy from groups. Karen was an introvert who *lost* energy in groups. Third, I didn't do the cooking so I was free to invite folks over to eat. Karen, who had to do the cooking, preferred knowing in advance if we were hosting guests for a meal. All of these differences caused great conflict, and our miscommunication made it worse.

Over the last 30 years or so we've learned to accept, appreciate and affirm our differences. We've also worked hard to compliment and support each other. I'm still an extrovert, but I now get my fellowship needs met without destroying Karen's quiet times. The way we got out of the downward spiral of despair was through the training and application of the tools and skills explained in this book. They've been life savers for my family and for me.

For better or for worse, the principle Kettering pointed out almost 50 years ago remains just as true today. Most communication problems will never be solved by mechanical technology because they stem from the human obstacles within us. Human nature and the subjective filters we use to decode and interpret what others say make us easy prey to the frustrating communication barriers we've discussed in this chapter. Overcoming these barriers requires a new approach to human relationships, one that guides us in the ways of the Spirit and teaches us in the ways of the heart. Such a helping model is exactly what we're proposing.

Before getting into the *teleios* helping model, let's look at a few specific behavior patterns that can cause great pain in relationships as well as acting as barriers to good communication.

Adverse Advice

No issue in communication causes more controversy than advice giving.

Although Charlie Steinmetz is not a household name among non-scientists, it is in the field of scientific research and technology. As the story goes, Charlie described himself as an immigrant blessed with an "electronic mind." He used his unique gifts to build the electrical generators for Henry Ford's first plant in Dearborn, Michigan.

One day, those generators failed to function, causing plant production to come to a halt. Ordinary mechanics and electricians were brought in to analyze and solve the problem, but to no avail. Henry Ford was losing money and lots of it. And Henry hated losing money.

Desperate to resume production, Ford called in Steinmetz. The genius arrived and immediately began to tinker around with some of the circuits. First he tinkered with one part then another. Meanwhile, Ford's employees stood in disbelief at the seeming incompetence of this man who appeared to be doing nothing more than fooling around. After a few hours of jiggling here and messing around there, Steinmetz threw the main generator switch and power was instantly restored.

Returning home, the electronics wizard forwarded a bill to Henry Ford for $10,000.

Although an extremely wealthy man, Ford viewed the amount as outrageous and returned the invoice to Steinmetz with the note: "Charlie, isn't this a little steep for a few hours of tinkering?"

Steinmetz, the story goes, reworked the bill and sent it back to Ford. This time it read: "$10 for tinkering around. $9,990 for knowing where to tinker. Total: $10,000."

Henry Ford paid the bill.

The point is obvious. Understanding where, how and when to offer specific help or advice requires discernment, insight, knowledge and skill. All of us have experienced situations where we asked for help, only to receive unwanted or unhealthy advice instead of the wisdom and insight that was needed. As a boy in school, I was full of questions and curiosity about every subject and topic we ever covered in class. In many instances I would ask a good question, only to receive a good answer to a different question.

The key to successful helping is accurate, wise advice. Unfortunately, well-meaning friends and relatives can become what I call *adverse advisors* when they offer canned or unwise advice that might be a good answer to a question that is not being asked. And *people rarely listen to answers to questions they haven't asked.*

Adverse Advisors

These folks may mean well, but their "helping" can have the opposite of its intended effect. Let's take a look at the most common adverse advisors and their various responses to an everyday problem — a toothache. (If you see yourself among these folks, just smile and realize that you have lots of company.)

Here's the scenario. Imagine that you woke up this morning with a terrible toothache. Even though you're in real pain, you decide to go to work anyway. As the day wears on, the pain becomes excruciating — so much so that your co-workers can't help noticing your discomfort. So along they come, each with their own unique approaches to being "helpful."

The Interrogator

This is the guy (or gal) who wants *"The facts, Ma'am. Just the facts."* He bores in with a barrage of questions until we begin to wonder if the bright light and rubber hose are coming out next.

When did your tooth start hurting?

Which tooth is it?

Where were you when it started hurting?

Did you bite down on something hard?

How many times has this happened before?

Who's your dentist?

The General

Here's the person who likes to give orders, directions and commands to help you straighten out the "mess" you're making out of your life.

Call the dentist right away and demand an appointment! Today!

Tell him he must see you immediately. Don't take no for an answer.

You must get that tooth taken care of without delay. Quick! Get to a phone. Call him now!

The Pharisee

This is the perennial accuser, always ready to shake a finger at you. If you have a problem, it's your own fault. No question about it!

You should have taken better care of your teeth! Don't you realize that your body is God's temple?

If you'd brushed and flossed regularly, you wouldn't be paying the consequences now!

See! That's what comes from eating all those candy bars.

The Labeler

This person seems to believe that if your problem can be categorized, labeled and pigeonholed, everything will be just fine. The Labeler loves to use the latest buzz words and jargon.

You know what? I just bet you have Temporal Mandibular Joint Syndrome. That's what's causing your toothache. When you have TMJ, it's perfectly normal to have different teeth ache at different times. Yep! That's what you've got all right! I just know it.

The Prophet

This seemingly clairvoyant advisor delights in predicting a future full of gloom and doom for you.

You know. . . You probably have an abscess and they'll have to either do a root canal or remove it altogether! And once they remove one, it's really hard to attach the new one to your existing teeth; but if they do, that sometimes causes your other teeth to rot. Then the whole process just starts all over again. I hate to tell you, but this could just be the beginning of your problems.

The Historian

This lovable character is filled with stories of similar experiences and just can't wait to tell you all about them.

Boy, the last time I had a bad toothache, it took six weeks for them to figure out what to do. It was just awful! I went to four specialists and they finally decided I should have all my teeth pulled and wear dentures. That was about three years ago and since then I. . .

The Quick Change Artist

The Quick Change Artist switches the subject smoothly, using your problem as a jumping-off point.

Speaking of dentists, my uncle is a dentist. He lives in Colorado where we had vacationed last summer. You know, that was one of the best vacations we ever had. Really! The mountains are so beautiful and the hiking is great.

Dr. Deodorant

This "doc" can't stand unpleasantness in any form. Fortunately for you, he has the solution. Just cover up the discomfort with sweet smelling words.

You are such a nice person and do such nice things for people. It just isn't fair that you should have such an awful toothache. But I'm sure everything will turn out fine.

Grandma Chicken Soup

A first cousin to Dr. Deodorant, this advisor tries to make problems disappear with kindly actions rather than words. And the action usually starts in the kitchen.

I'm sure it's hard to chew, so why don't I run home at lunch and fix you up some nice broth to drink until you can get to the dentist? I'll make a casserole for your family and some soup for you. And I'll rent you a video, too. That way you can watch it and not think about your tooth. Here, in the meantime, just sip on this cup of hot tea. It'll make it feel all better.

Miss Bumper Sticker

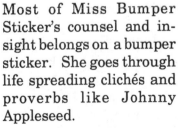

Most of Miss Bumper Sticker's counsel and insight belongs on a bumper sticker. She goes through life spreading clichés and proverbs like Johnny Appleseed.

Remember, all things work together for good!

When life gives you lemons, make lemonade!

God helps those who help themselves!

After all, no pain, no gain!

The Robber

He *knows* exactly how you feel before taking time to listen to you. He literally robs you of an opportunity to speak for yourself and steals your emotion from you.

I know just how you feel! The pain and all the frustration is incredible!

Your jaw hurts, your head aches, and your whole body is one giant nerve. You just want to go home.

Recognize anyone you know? Or possibly you see a little bit of yourself in some of these? At one time or another, most of us have resorted to "quick and dirty" advice-giving or "band-aiding" another's problem as a way of avoiding our own pain. Adverse advisors, in fact, skillfully avoid genuine involvement and communication that touches on deep-heart issues. They usually shut down, gloss over and/or run away from any interaction that gets too "real" for them to deal with comfortably.

Grace-Based Helping

The adverse advisors develop in our lives as a result of our temperament and experiences as well as the way we learned to "help others." Some people learn that the adverse advisors are the preferred mode of helping. But we suggest what we call "grace-based helping," an approach which encourages people to listen carefully with love and acceptance (grace) prior to offering any advice or wisdom at all.

Grace-based helping encourages the helper to be genuinely concerned about the person seeking assistance and to prefer

64

the quality of the relationship over the quality of the advice. Grace-full helping accepts people as they are with no condemnation or disrespect.

Although we know that grace is necessary to become an effective helper, we can't change our attitudes without a great deal of work. "But," you say, "isn't grace from God? And don't I receive it freely from the Lord?"

Indeed, God's grace is free; and it's life changing. But old habits of the mind and heart die slowly. Several years ago I complained to a Christian mentor that "growing in the Lord shouldn't require so much discipline and hard work." "It should," I said, "happen naturally." The mentoring pastor gave me an answer that continues to stick in my head: "Well, Gary, the only thing that happens naturally in humans is Sin. Everything else requires a combination of hard work and God's power."

A good model is the one followed by the Franciscans in France so many years ago when they were reclaiming wasteland for farming. They called it *Ora et Labora* in Latin. We call it prayer and work. In the Jesus Movement of the '70s we said it this way: *"Work as if everything depends on you and pray as if everything depends upon God"*.

Now that we have looked at some of the problems and barriers, we are ready for a helping model that works. The next chapter explains our *teleios* approach to helping.

6

Climbing Mount Everest

If you've ever traveled across America's heartland, you may have discovered "Mt. Sunflower." You won't find it in your *Rand McNally Road Atlas*. Travel bureaus have probably never heard of it. Still, it has a distinction all its own. A modest sign sums it up: "Mt. Sunflower, the highest mountain in Kansas." Mt. Sunflower may be nothing more than the handiwork of a farmer with a good sense of humor; but for me, Mt. Sunflower is symbolic of something more.

Many people try to tackle the besetting problems in their lives all at once. They're like rookies trying to ascend Mt. Everest. They just don't have the understanding or experience in mountain climbing necessary to reach the summit.

Those who make it up Mt. Everest generally start out slowly. They first find an experienced guide who assists them in learning basic safety measures and mountaineering skills. Then they spend time climbing the low elevations with dedication until they learn to handle all of the challenges and obstacles; and, finally, they make it to the top. After years of climbing and learning, the student may be able to become a teacher and help others learn to climb mountains, too.

Those who try to skip the beginning or the in-between steps and undertake the climb alone or unprepared can get into real trouble. Some merely give up in frustration and disillusionment when confronted with the hardships of the climb. Others are killed or permanently scarred by the experience. In any case, without mastering the basics, we will never become master climbers and reach the summit.

Helpers and Seekers

A **Helper** is any individual willing to assist others in the process of moving toward growth, change or healing. As we explore the difficult and complicated terrain of our inner selves and tackle the towering obstacles confronting us in our journey toward wholeness, helpers come alongside us to listen, encourage, counsel and exhort.

A **Seeker** is anyone desiring to grow by pursuing help, greater understanding or personal involvement. We avoid the terms client, patient and counselee because they imply that the Seeker is a passive recipient instead of an active participant in the quest for healing. In a true process of growth, nothing could be further from the truth.

It may surprise you to learn that these roles are interchangeable. At different times any one of us can be either a Helper or a Seeker. Training in listening and caring skills will help us in both roles.

We all need help in conquering our personal Mt. Everests, and the first step is to learn an effective and safe process for pursuing change. If we're wise, we'll begin with something a little less demanding than the Rockies or Everest. . . like Mt. Sunflower.

To tackle the emotional and behavioral mountains or molehills in your life, or to help others do so, you need a workable plan of attack. This chapter will describe such a plan and the fundamental process for bringing about helpful change in people's lives. We call this plan the *teleios* model of helping. You may be eager to get started, but let's slow down and look at the best way to help others begin the climbing process. Then we can focus on learning how to scale the peaks.

The most important task of a Helper or guide is to clearly understand and articulate the exact nature of the climber's needs. For example, Helpers cannot give expert "advice" until they know the level of experience, training, insight and talents of the person they're helping as well as where that individual wants to go. As a professional helper, I often draw on my years as a coach to remind me just how important it is to understand the readiness of a player before I offer coaching insight.

Insight and Action

To illustrate this idea, let me share an episode from the days when I was coaching elementary school basketball. Vernon was on the "B" team and early in the season was just learning how to play the game. Not only was he inexperienced, he was also one of the youngest and smallest players on the squad. Late in the fourth quarter of a game that we were winning easily, I decided to put Vernon into the game so he could get some actual game experience. Since we had spent very little time in practice, I attempted to give Vernon some critical information about his role.

"You guard number 14," I told Vernon. "If he gets the ball, whatever you do, DON'T LET HIM SHOOT!" I thought that those instructions were simple, straightforward and impossible to misunderstand. Well, sure enough, in a magnificent turnover play, number 14 took the ball and went charging down the court with Vernon in hot pursuit. To my amazement, when number 14 began to put the ball up on the backboard, highly motivated but confused and inexperienced little Vernon proceeded to hit him — hard! — right in the middle of the back. Within seconds, both were lying unmoving on the floor.

In astonishment and apprehension, the opposing coach and I both rushed to the end of the court to tend to the two wounded boys who, fortunately, only had the wind knocked out of their sails and weren't seriously injured. As soon as Vernon was able to orient himself, he looked up at me from that gym floor, his brown eyes wide in a look of bewilderment, and told me, "I done what you said, Mr. Sweeten. I didn't let him shoot!"

I learned an important lesson from Vernon that day. In issuing him a purely verbal command, I expected my young player to *act* without *insight*. And that's exactly what he did. He acted without fully understanding the rules of the game or what I really wanted. Had we spent more time in practice so Vernon could develop some insight before putting him into the game, the outcome would have been far different.

As we discovered in the last two chapters, because there are so many barriers to accurate and effective interpersonal relationships, caring Helpers, like coaches, need a specific plan and process to follow to avoid making the same mistakes I made with Vernon. For example, I really knew in my head that Vernon needed to rehearse being a defensive player many times in practice before he was forced to implement it in the pressure of a real game; but I got impatient and jumped ahead to action before Vernon had the insight and skills to do what I said. Had I followed my coaching plan, the near disaster would never have occurred; although Vernon might have been upset with me for not putting him into the game.

The plan and process outlined here is based on the Helper's being able to follow the Spirit rather than give in to peer pressure or pressure from the Seeker. Our model rests on the fruit of peace, patience, love and faith in God rather than on pressure to perform. So take a deep breath and read on.

The purpose of coaching is to help the players and the team. The purpose of relational helping is to minister to the needs of the Seeker. Any time a coach or a Helper becomes overly concerned with his own reputation, his own ego needs or his own fame, the players or Seekers suffer. The focus of the *teleios* helping model is aimed like a laser beam on helping others discover effective ways to grow into health.

Caution Lights

Every day we rely on an extremely simple safety device. It's very commonly used and prevents countless accidents and injuries around the world. Perhaps you have guessed that it's a traffic light. The familiar green, yellow and red signal is a helpful tool for teaching a universal process for encouraging healthy growth and change. Because we're ministering to the upside-down heart mentioned in Chapter 2, we're using an upside-down traffic light.

The traffic light provides a great way to remember the stages of a helping relationship. Robert R. Carkhuff,[1] Gerard Egan,[2] my friend Richard Walters[3] and several others have researched the differences between effective and ineffective Helpers. What they found is both exciting and hopeful. It seems that effective Helpers, whether professional or lay, have certain characteristics (called "core conditions" by Carkhuff) that ineffective Helpers do not possess.

There are four distinct phases in effective Helping. Our symbolic traffic light guides us systematically through the Carkhuff core conditions of warmth, empathy, respect, genuineness, concreteness, self-disclosure, confrontation and immediacy. Each colored signal adds a specific group of *core conditions* necessary for facilitating insight and taking effective action. Our *teleios* helping model incorporates a balanced theological approach as well as an internationally proven emotional growth process. The beauty of this model is found in the fact that it presents a process for both healthy Helping and healthy Seeking.

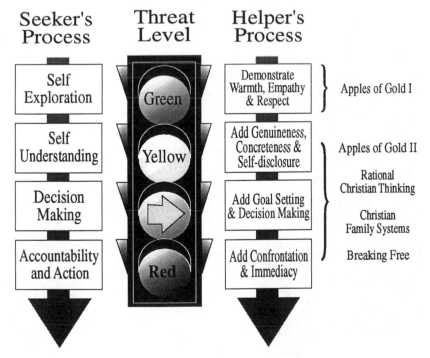

The green light represents Seeker self-exploration and trust building. In this first phase of the growth process, a Seeker explores confused or contradictory thoughts and feelings. By listening carefully while showing the attitudes and skills of warmth, empathy and respect, a friend can be an effective Helper and encourage the Seeker to move toward deeper self-understanding. The research of Carkhuff, et al., indicates that if we interact with the green light core conditions, then the people around us will grow toward health.

The yellow light represents the stage of self-understanding or insight. Once a Seeker has developed a trusting relationship with the Helper by thoroughly exploring his thoughts and feelings, he's ready to focus on specific insights which can lead to appropriate action steps. The Helper supports the process with warmth, empathy and respect and uses the skills of genuineness, concreteness and self-disclosure to "speak the truth in love." This enables the Seeker to discover the roots of his problem or dilemma.

The yellow arrow represents the decision-making phase. The Seeker now has enough insight to make good decisions, set appropriate goals and count the cost of changing his behavior. The Helper continues to show warmth, empathy, respect, genuineness, concreteness and self-disclosure, which assists the Seeker in his trek toward lasting and healthy change.

The red light phase represents effective action. The Seeker uses the power generated by the understanding and insight gained in the previous stages to translate decisions and plans into meaningful action steps. The Helper continues to provide both support and accountability by using all the core conditions. In addition the Helper can, when needed, practice confrontation and immediacy skills that challenge the Seeker to face the pain of change.

The process of helping is dynamic and the light can also go from red back to green because effective helping almost always opens up new areas for exploration, insight and action. I remember a Bible teacher telling our class back in 1974 how wonderfully this model was working for her. After learning about the traffic light and implementing the core conditions of warmth, empathy and respect, Nancy found that her students were opening up to her in deeply moving ways. "Once I discovered that I didn't have to solve all of their problems, they talked my arm off. And each week they came to class wanting to discuss not only the Bible, but how it could help them with their problems."

The foundational skills involved in every phase of the process are warmth, empathy and respect. These key skills are the focus of the next several chapters. The skills of genuineness, concreteness, self-disclosure, action, confrontation and immediacy are covered in the next book and class in the LIFE training series. Be assured, we *do* believe in action and accountability. The whole *teleios* model, in fact, is based on an equation suggested by Dr. Frank Lake, a British therapist and a Christian.

Care + Confrontation = Growth + Tribulation

The green light core conditions emphasize *care* or the tender fruit of the Spirit so essential to Christian helping. But care without action and accountability is terribly unloving because it does nothing to change the situation. So care without confrontation leads to minimum growth and minimum tribulation.

The yellow light, yellow arrow and red light sections of our *teleios* model emphasize confrontation by facing reality. Some Christian helping models begin here, but confrontation without compassion or caring leads to little growth and great tribulation.

The *teleios* traffic light provides a balanced approach to leadership, pastoring and parenting because all of the Biblical concepts and teachings are preserved but placed into a proper context. Beware of any model that presents a "nothing but" approach. "Counseling or parenting is *nothing but* loving. Don't ever discipline." Or, "Counseling or parenting is *nothing but* pointing out sin." In this book and this training you will learn one part of effective helping. It is a key part but not the only part that is needed.

Maximum Care + Maximum Confrontation = Maximum Growth + Maximum Tribulation

Growth pains are normal and to be desired. But make sure they arise from growth rather than from insensitive helping.

The Traffic Light In Action

To show the dynamic way this model works, Dave Ping shares from one of the most stressed-out periods in his life:

When I was working in the inner city, there was a time when I was feeling down in the dumps. One day I was talking to my friend Paul who was trained in the teleios *model of helping, and something happened that changed my life.*

Green Light

The way he listened made all of the difference. I started out talking about the vague sense of heaviness and sadness I was feeling. As he listened and reflected back what I was saying . . . I heard myself saying things I had never openly said before. This helped me face the fact that I wasn't just stressed out, I was deeply depressed.

My ministry was going well, but I felt like a failure. As I talked, pain began to well up from deep inside me, and I was surprised and a little embarrassed when the tears began to flow. His caring allowed me to see the truth and was the beginning of a deep healing in my life.

Yellow Light

Time passed and I began, with the help of Paul, to understand the roots of my feelings. One day it dawned on me that it wasn't my job that was causing the inner anguish. It was my underlying beliefs about myself. Paul helped me a great deal as I examined and challenged my old beliefs.

Yellow Arrow

I eventually came to the point where I knew that the false beliefs had to be changed. If I didn't change my stinkin' thinkin' I would never overcome my depression. I made up my mind and prayed for God to help me change. At that point, Paul again helped me work out specific steps for renewing my mind using Scripture in combination with Rational Christian Thinking.[4]

Red Light

Changing my beliefs turned out to be much harder than I thought. I felt like giving up lots of times, but Paul kept on encouraging me and challenging me to stick to my goals.

Over a period of about twelve months, Paul and the Lord helped me develop a renewed, rational thinking process and the long-term depression lifted.

What began as a simple conversation has yielded tremendous growth and healing — and none of it would have happened if my friend hadn't taken the time to listen, care and challenge me to change.

Dave describes the process as an ongoing spiral:

I kept working through the steps, but continually came back to the basic skills only at deeper and deeper levels. I was surprised how much Paul's warmth, true respect and skilled empathy helped me move through the painful areas of personal healing and growth. In fact, the process revealed that I had been depressed for years without realizing it. Now, although I'm certainly not immune to low periods for a day or two, that dark hole of depression has never returned – because a lay friend had learned some simple skills at church.

Anne's Story

Anne, the other co-author with Dave and Gary, shares a story to illustrate how this helping process worked for her. Once a smoker, Anne found it difficult to break the habit — until members of her Bible study began to use the *teleios* model in the group.

Green Light

Through worshipping together and sharing our lives to-gether, our small group had become very close. For a long time I was ashamed to admit to them that I still smoked cigarettes, so I hid my habit. As I began to see that they wouldn't reject or judge me, I was able to let the group know about my struggle to quit smoking. They were good listeners. As I put my thoughts and feelings into words, I realized that when I first started smoking, it was both to fit in with the crowd and to rebel against my mother's authority. Smoking was the one thing my mother disliked intensely.

Yellow Light

As I talked about it further, I realized that I still had some real hurt in relation to Mother. I grew up believing that she didn't really accept me because she wanted a son instead of a third daughter. I was occasionally introduced with the words, "This is our son." As I examined my thoughts and feelings closely, I understood that the hurt and my smoking problem were closely related.

Yellow Arrow

This insight led me to decide to give up both the smoking and the hurt feelings. As a result, the group helped me make a plan to accomplish those goals. They also prayed and supported me emotionally through the process. By listening and sharing some of their own struggles with me, they encouraged me to grow in self-awareness and find the courage to move toward change.

Red Light

The first goal was to forgive my mother for the ways she had unintentionally hurt me. As I prayed for God's help in that area, I was set free to quit smoking. Later a member of the group encouraged me to talk with Mother about my feelings, but I resisted the idea because I didn't want her to feel guilty. Finally, I mustered up the courage to share my insights with her and I was surprised by her reaction.

Mother admitted that as a young woman, she felt the same way as I did. She thought that her mother was partial to her brothers. Both of us recognized how our family belief that boys are more important had caused us pain. The conversation was extremely healing for both of us. As we talked, I gained more insight and realized that I was sending negative signals to my four daughters. This led me to ask forgiveness from them and to begin to relate to them in an even deeper, more genuine, way.

And so the spiraling process continued. Anne thought her problem was smoking. The shame she felt about it had kept her in bondage. So once the group began to listen non-judgmentally, she began to see a connection between an external habit and an internal hurt.

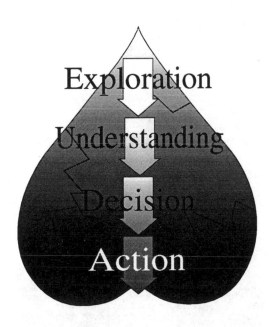

Exploring those hurts led to a discussion that revealed even deeper dynamics and opened up new ways to grow. Finally, Anne decided to change the way she parented the four girls in her family. This is a long stretch from a smoking problem but exactly the kind of process that the *teleios* model encourages.

Reflect for a moment what might have happened to Dave or Anne had they met up with one or more of the Adverse Advisors rather than a healthy Helper. Would the outcome of a long-term depression be the same for Dave had he encountered the Bumper Sticker? Would Anne have been able not only to stop smoking but also to resolve a family issue of generations if she had met the Pharisee? And what about you? Would you prefer to share your deep heart with someone who labels you, or with a *teleios* Helper?

The *teleios* model (both the plan and the process) is consciously designed to minister to the whole person with the whole Scripture. As you can see from the above examples, we often work with people who begin their stories with a rather simple or straightforward "problem," but it connects to something more complex, deeper or hidden. The upside-down heart described in Chapter 2 illustrates that it's important to have a model that enables us to handle "superficial" issues as well as those that come from deep within.

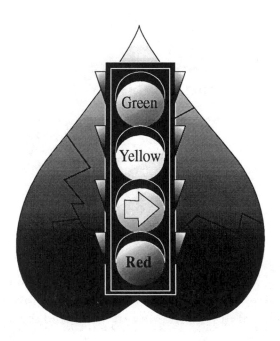

The *teleios* traffic light system corresponds to the various levels of feeling, thought, memory and experience contained in the heart. The green light core conditions focus on the issues surfaced by the Seeker. The Helper shows warmth, empathy and respect for whatever the Seeker says. As the conversation proceeds, so does the intensity of feeling and the depth of the memories that are revealed. Thus, the yellow light signals "Caution: Slow down!" Moving through an intersection on a yellow light calls for extreme caution, so we want to make sure that any action steps that are prescribed are the correct ones. Finally, the red light makes sure that we have stopped, looked and listened before confronting someone's behavior. The red light also symbolizes the level of anxiety of a Seeker on any experience.

Proportional Helping

Dave has developed another graphic to illustrate that warmth, empathy and respect make up proportionately at least three-fourths of the *teleios* model. As you can see, mastering these three skills first is the foundation to later effectiveness.

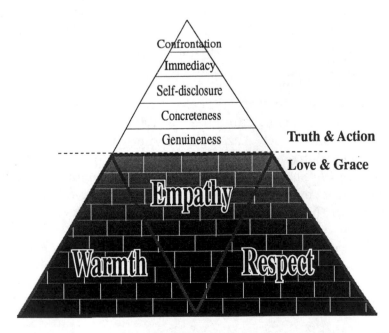

I have my own yellow flashing light of caution at this point. There are many books on "inner healing" and Christian counseling being sold by the millions to people who do not understand the skill it takes to minister to the deep heart. Some of these books even give step-by-step instructions for healing the deep wounds of abuse, trauma and rejection. This is what I call "Karaoke Christian Counseling" because people "sing along with a tape" to bring healing and deliverance. This is a very dangerous thing to do.

I once told a famous author of books on inner healing that he was turning people loose with dynamite that could be lethal. After that, he began to train lay counselors to spend more time listening than performing open heart surgery. Still, the books, tapes and manuals abound, encouraging people to be heart surgeons when they have never learned the basic anatomy of the heart.

As believers, we see the heart of another human being as the "Holy of Holies," where the Spirit of God resides. Those of us who dare to draw near must, like Moses, take off our shoes, for we are treading on holy ground. The priest did not rush into the Holy of Holies, lest he be struck dead. Instead, he prepared carefully and slowly to approach God. So must we go slowly into the deep heart of a child of God. Don't rush in and disturb the Spirit. Go gently and bring peace.

Now that we have attempted to lay a firm foundation, we will begin to examine each piece of the helping plan and process. The first piece is learning to show friendship and warmth to those around you. Although moving quickly to action or confrontation may be tempting, the Carkhuff research is clear that they are not as important to long-term health as the core conditions more closely related to the fruit of peace and patience. Nor is it as efficient to skip this part.

Taking more time initially to listen and love actually speeds up the helping process. As a therapist, my key job is to try to understand what a client is saying, feeling and thinking. If I miss on that part, I can't hit on the action part.

How do we know when to move from the green to the yellow to the red phases?

Ask yourself the following questions:

Green Light

Has the Seeker fully explored his thoughts and feelings and come to some new insights?

If so, he is ready to move to the yellow light.

If not, continue using warmth, respect and empathy.

Yellow Light

Has the Seeker closely examined his new insight from several different points of view?

If so, he is ready to move on to goal setting or the yellow arrow phase.

If not, continue using warmth, empathy, respect, concreteness, genuineness and self-disclosure only.

Yellow Arrow

Has the Seeker set healthy goals and chosen options for change?

If so, he is ready to move to the red light phase of accountability and action.

If not, continue using warmth, empathy, respect, concreteness, genuineness, self-disclosure and goal setting skills.

Red Light

Has the Seeker taken steps toward healthier living?

If so, he may be ready to move on into other areas of growth or terminate the helping process.

If not, continue using warmth, empathy, respect, concreteness, genuineness, self-disclosure, goal setting, confrontation and immediacy.

As you can see, warmth, empathy and respect are crucial to all four levels of deep-heart helping. As the chart on the next page demonstrates, healthy relationships are built and sustained on a foundation of these three skills. We will begin our next chapter by focusing on warmth.

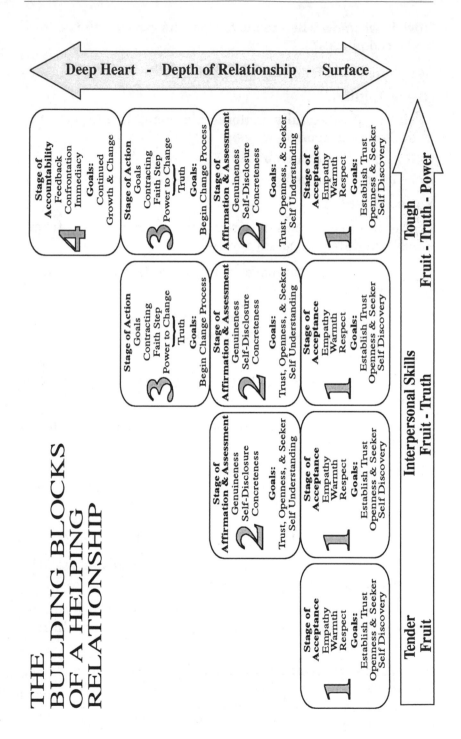

THE
BUILDING BLOCKS
OF A HELPING
RELATIONSHIP

Deep Heart - Depth of Relationship - Surface

Stage of Accountability
Feedback
Confrontation
Immediacy
Goals:
Continued
Growth & Change
4

Stage of Action
Goals
Contracting
Faith Step
Power to Change
Truth
Goals:
Begin Change Process
3

Stage of Affirmation & Assessment
Genuineness
Self-Disclosure
Concreteness
Goals:
Trust, Openness, & Seeker
Self Understanding
2

Stage of Acceptance
Empathy
Warmth
Respect
Goals:
Establish Trust
Openness & Seeker
Self Discovery
1

Stage of Action
Goals
Contracting
Faith Step
Power to Change
Truth
Goals:
Begin Change Process
3

Stage of Affirmation & Assessment
Genuineness
Self-Disclosure
Concreteness
Goals:
Trust, Openness, & Seeker
Self Understanding
2

Stage of Acceptance
Empathy
Warmth
Respect
Goals:
Establish Trust
Openness & Seeker
Self Discovery
1

Stage of Affirmation & Assessment
Genuineness
Self-Disclosure
Concreteness
Goals:
Trust, Openness, & Seeker
Self Understanding
2

Stage of Acceptance
Empathy
Warmth
Respect
Goals:
Establish Trust
Openness & Seeker
Self Discovery
1

Stage of Acceptance
Empathy
Warmth
Respect
Goals:
Establish Trust
Openness & Seeker
Self Discovery
1

Tough
Fruit - Truth - Power

Interpersonal Skills
Fruit - Truth

Tender
Fruit

SOLAR TEA

Isn't it funny how a simple cup of coffee or tea offered by a caring and hospitable person can make us feel welcome and comfortable — especially if we've just come in from the cold?

Or on a scorching summer day. . . how inviting a pitcher of cool lemonade or backyard-brewed solar tea can be.

Whenever I think of solar tea, I think of Emmy. Even at age 88, she was the soul of hospitality. She really knew how to put me at ease and help me feel welcome in her modest home. She would greet me at the door with a genuine smile, wrapping her frail arms around me in a warm hug and, of course, always insisting that I share a cup or glass of tea: stove-top brewed and boiling hot in the winter, naturally sun-brewed out on the back porch and poured over ice in the summer.

There was something special about sharing a glass of tea with Emmy. For some reason it just always tasted better at her place. I'm sure it had nothing to do with the brand of tea bags she used or how much sugar or lemon she added. No, I think it had more to do with Emmy herself. She knew how to communicate love and caring in an extraordinary way.

Emmy's been gone for some time now, but every time I think of her I can still feel her personal warmth.

Maybe you know someone like Emmy who has a gift for helping you feel welcome and accepted. Somehow when you're around them you feel — well, important! Like what's on your mind is deeply significant. Without saying much of anything, they can communicate interest and caring love. Can you think of a person who has communicated this special kind of love and caring to you? What adjectives would you use in describing him or her? Chances are *warmth* will be among your word choices.

Warmth, or *communicating caring love,* is more often demonstrated by subtle mannerisms, actions and facial expressions than by words. A gentle look, a warm smile or an inviting gesture can express acceptance more quickly and deeply than words. Such nonverbals, working together with voice tone, inflection and actual words, can project friendliness, consideration and warmth.

According to studies conducted by UCLA researcher Professor Albert Mehrabian, actual words make up only seven percent of our interpersonal communications. The remaining 93% is communicated through nonverbal signals and voice tone.[1]

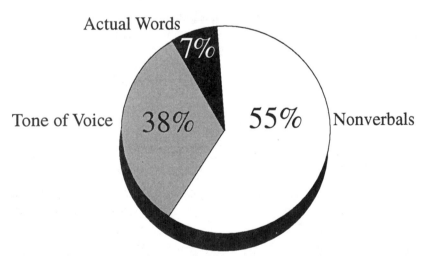

Actual Words 7%

Tone of Voice 38%   55% Nonverbals

Nonverbals and Voice Tone are 93% of Communication

Even the most conservative studies estimate that from 55% to 65% of our communication is nonverbal. If this is so, then why is it that most of us are concerned with "saying the right thing"? It's much simpler to demonstrate a caring attitude by paying attention to our nonverbals. They may even be the most important part of our interpersonal communication because nonverbals are the first thing people look for.

Emmy never went beyond the eighth grade. She was never schooled in "letters" or in semantics, but she didn't have to rely on proper word choice and usage to communicate the fact that she genuinely cared about me. Her interest and concern were obvious because she was so warm.

Now you may be thinking: "I'm just not a naturally warm person. You can't learn something like that. You're either born with it or you're not."

But that's not true. You can develop personal and relational warmth — no matter who you are. Learning the basics is actually fairly simple. The challenge comes in developing attitudes and practicing the skills that communicate that caring to others. Fortunately, as we work on developing these helpful qualities, we can count on help from the Holy Spirit.

Galatians 5:22 and 23 tell us that "the fruit of the Spirit is love, joy, peace, patience, kindness, goodness, faithfulness, gentleness and self-control." To me these qualities sound a lot like the kind of warmth I experienced from Emmy. She combined a loving attitude with actions that communicated caring.

Engaging Others

From a spiritual perspective, warmth is very important. Think for a moment about Jesus. What was there about Him that allowed people to feel so secure, so loved and accepted in His presence? We don't really know what He looked like, but I imagine there was something about His eyes, His face and His attentiveness to people that conveyed caring and love. The Jesus of the Gospels is a very warm person whose caring is apparent in His actions and in the way people respond to Him.

85

In Matthew 19:13, for example, we find people spontaneously taking their little children to Jesus and asking Him to bless and pray for them. Over the objections of His schedule-conscious disciples, Jesus said, "Let the little children come to Me, and do not hinder them, for the kingdom of heaven belongs to such as these" (Matthew 19:14).

Isn't this a wonderful picture? Jesus with little children sitting on his knees. Children might not always understand theology, but they can sense genuine warmth and caring. They can also sense when people are "talking the talk without walking the walk." While vacationing in Florida, I went to hear an evangelist speak. He told of a time when he was invited to preach at a large church on the topic of love. At the very beginning of the sermon, the evangelist shouted while pointing a finger at the congregation, "You should love like Jesus loved!"

A hush fell over all the people except for a four-year-old in the front row. Startled by the loud voice, she turned to the adult next to her and said in a loud voice: "Let's get out of here, Grandma. That guy is mad at everybody!" This comment from a little child so challenged the evangelist that he decided he had better learn a lot more about love before preaching on it.

In ministering to the little children, Jesus spoke a message that went far beyond mere words. Children knew immediately that they were important and that they were loved. This is only one example. Throughout His earthly ministry, Jesus interacted warmly with people and was able to break down the barriers of fear to engage with people on a heart-to-heart level.

This is what warmth does. It engages. It invites. It opens doors. It laughs. It encourages *childlikeness* rather than *childishness*.

Throughout the scriptures we're reminded to follow the model of Jesus by showing warmth and compassion toward one another. Paul also reminds us in Romans 12:10, "Love one another warmly as Christian brothers and be eager to show respect for one another" (Good News Bible, Today's English Version).

86

The high value Scripture places on warmth is also eloquently depicted in one of my favorite passages from the Old Testament, Psalm 103: 2-4:

> *Praise the Lord, Oh my soul, and forget not all His benefits — Who forgives all your sins and heals all your diseases, Who redeems your life from the pit and crowns you with love and compassion.*

We praise God for forgiveness, healing and redemption; but the *coup de gras*, the finishing touch, is a crown of love and compassion.

Since the Bible clearly encourages us to be warm and compassionate, it's not all that surprising that research also shows that personal warmth is one of three qualities we most need to effectively help others. The other two are empathy and respect, and they'll be discussed in the next two chapters.

Robert R. Carkhuff found that the people most effective in helping others are able to communicate warmth and caring to others.[2] Numerous studies show that warmth breaks down barriers and helps overcome much of the resistance to healthy change we described in the chapter on communication barriers. When the New Testament writers use the term "brotherly [or sisterly] love," they employ the Greek word *phileo*, referring to true tenderness, warmth and friendliness between people.

In his book *How To Be A People Helper*,[3] Christian psychologist Dr. Gary Collins explains how genuine warmth and caring cause lay helpers to be even more effective in many situations than are counseling professionals. While professionals are sometimes cold or clinical, caring friends can communicate authentic warmth and caring in a way that encourages hurting people toward health. Modern scientific study confirms Dr. Collins' conclusions about the importance of warmth in relationships. A few of the studies follow:

The Journal of Family Issues (June, 1990)[4], states that "the fostering of warmth within the parent-child relationship may be able to decrease drug and alcohol use in early adolescence." (Caring love helps to avoid a multitude of problems.)

Social Behavior and Personality, (volume 18, 1990)[5] reports that the appearance of "parental warmth and family cohesion" are significant predictors of a child's self-esteem. (Caring love helps to build positive self-esteem.)

Psychological Reports' (April, 1990)[6] findings indicate that warmth is significantly related to the social, emotional and cognitive functioning of at-risk youngsters. (Caring love enhances the health and education of kids.)

Childhood Education Journal (winter, 1988)[7] states that cognitive growth can be enhanced by attending to the level of emotional warmth between teacher and child. (Caring love helps children reach their full potential.)

A German study (reported in *Psychologie-in-Erziehung-und-Unterricht,* volume 34, 1987)[8] suggests that a kindergarten teacher's emotional warmth is correlated with motor activity and stimulation of the child's development. (A teacher's caring love helps the physical development of children.)

In addition to the Bible, professional journals and medical theories, the significance of warm, loving nonverbals also receives lots of attention these days in newspapers and popular magazines.

The April 1991 issue of *Working Woman* features an article ("The Subtle Signs of Success"[9]) emphasizing the importance of nonverbal communication. In it, author Nancy Austin writes that being aware of nonverbal communication can help people in business get their message across and avoid misunderstandings. As a consultant to business and industry, I can tell you in no uncertain terms that interpersonal warmth is a badly needed part of workplace communication. Medical schools are now training physicians in how to communicate warmth to their patients because doctors are less likely to be sued for malpractice when their "bedside manner" is warm and caring.

Perhaps the most important place to express *phileo* love (warmth) is at home. More than 80% of all family conflicts can be traced back to poor communication and a deficiency in the ability to express warmth and caring.[10] Most of us know intuitively that being warm is preferable, but we are unaware of how to improve our ability to communicate appropriate warmth and caring. Well, now you can get feedback on your level of warmth and learn how to increase it.

Regardless of how warm or cold you may seem to others now, you can learn how to improve your self-awareness by using the *Warmthometer* scale, on page 100 of this chapter.

To begin the process, it's important that we learn to recognize nonverbal signals and mannerisms in others, then work for awareness of what we're "saying" without words. A closer look at two forms of nonverbal communication will assist us in better understanding the signals we send and receive.

Nonverbal Clues

The mouth, head, face, shoulders, arms, legs, feet — the total body — provide a wealth of clues about what's going on inside our heads and hearts, about our feelings, about our inner states of being. Most of us read these signals in others without having to think about them. For example:

- Sagging shoulders tend to project a feeling of discouragement, exhaustion, despair or depression.

- Arms folded tightly across the chest tend to give the impression of defensiveness, impatience or alienation.

- Clenched hands and jaw may suggest anger or anguish.

- A quivering chin can suggest a struggle with intense emotion.

- Fidgeting and foot tapping may indicate nervousness and anxiety.

These nonverbal signals are usually obvious in others, but are often difficult to detect in ourselves. Good communicators and effective Helpers have learned to become sensitive to what they communicate through posture and body movement. Helpful Helpers are especially tuned in to these signals because physical mannerisms that we're not aware of sending can be distracting and annoying to others when we're in the role of Helper.

For example, a counselor friend of mine had a bad habit of looking at his wrist watch every few minutes while we were talking with each other — so much so that I had a difficult time believing that he was really listening. I finally got so frustrated that I told him how irritating and exasperating his clock watching was to me. Curiously enough, he was totally unaware that he had been doing it.

There are many other nonverbal habits that can detract from your warmth when you're listening to someone:

- Playing with an object such as a wedding band, button or paper clip.
- Twisting or playing with hair or clothing.
- Looking out of the window instead of at the speaker.
- Rocking back and forth in your chair.
- Sighing, yawning, or scratching.

I'm sure you can think of many more nonverbal villains — those unconscious, automatic behaviors that can steal your warmth. If you want to discover your hidden habits, close friends and spouses are usually more aware of these subtle mannerisms and may be willing to give you feedback if you ask.

Voice Clues

Another key to communicating personal warmth is our voice. Research shows the volume, pitch and tone of our voice comprise up to 38% of what we communicate.[11] All of us, in fact, have learned to intuitively listen for these voice qualities as clues to the real meaning of a person's words. Where we place the emphasis can also make a world of difference in the message we convey. Look at the following example:

"*I* didn't say your outfit looked silly."
Implication: *Someone else said it was silly.*

"I didn't **say** your outfit looked silly."
Implication: *I may have thought it was silly, but I didn't say so.*

"I didn't say **your** outfit looked silly."
Implication: *It wasn't you I was talking about.*

"I didn't say your **outfit** looked silly."
Implication: *It wasn't your outfit that looked silly. It was you.*

"I didn't say your outfit looked **silly**."
Implication: *I didn't say silly exactly. I said it looked unusual.*

Volume and pitch can also make a big difference in communicating warmth. What kind of impression do you get, for instance, from a person whose voice is fast and high-pitched? Nervous? Uptight? Antsy? Changes in volume and pitch can also reveal such emotions as fear, excitement, embarrassment or pride.

When you think of a warm voice, what are the qualities that come to mind? A voice that communicates caring and interest is usually low and soft, but clearly audible. Instead of being a monotone, it's rich in inflection and variation, reflecting the energy and mood of the other person.

You may have been aware of many of these things before you ever picked up this book, but it helps to spell it out in an orderly fashion. So here's our recipe for communicating caring love or warmth to those with whom you interact. Actually, it's as simple as making SOLAR TEA!

Sensitive Seating
Openness
Leaning
Appropriate Eye Contact
Relaxation

Touch
Environmental Awareness
Accommodating Attitude

Like any good recipe, there's nothing legalistic about this formula for improving warmth. As you read about each aspect of our SOLAR TEA acrostic, remember that each of us is a unique person. Naturally, we must all adapt these basic principles to our own personalities and cultures. With this in mind, let's take a closer look at the ingredients of SOLAR TEA.

Sensitive Seating

Believe it or not, the seating or standing positions we assume in person-to-person communication send strong nonverbal messages and set the tone for the interaction.

Recently, I was asked to evaluate a therapist in training. Positioned behind a one-way mirror, I was able to observe his interaction with the clients — a couple whose marriage was in obvious need of repair. Grasping his clip board like a security blanket, the young therapist sat about six feet away from the couple. The husband and wife were also understandably anxious and intimidated by his cold and distant approach.

My feedback to him was that he could improve his effectiveness dramatically by moving from his cool clinical posture into a warmer caring position. I suggested he "lose" the clip board and move to a more inviting distance about an arm's length away from the couple.

If you desire to communicate caring and acceptance, it's usually most comfortable and effective to sit face-to-face with the other person, but with your body positioned at about a 45-

degree angle. In other words, you don't want to face the other person "head on" in a position that's too confrontive, stiff or stilted.

When standing, this angled position is also the most natural and most inviting. While we often begin conversations with people while we're standing up, remaining standing through-out a conversation usually inhibits warmth. If possible, find a place where you can sit and talk. You'll see how this lowers tension and defensiveness.

Openness

Emotional and spiritual openness to others is communicated primarily through our posture and body language.

Sitting or standing with your arms crossed while engaged in a conversation with others often sends definite nonverbal smoke signals that are interpreted as a standoffish or distant attitude — or even one of disregard or apathy. Crossing your legs so that one leg becomes a barrier between you and the person you're talking with also lowers the Seeker's perception of your warmth.

When the question of leg crossing comes up in our LIFE seminars, I usually recommend keeping your feet on the floor because it promotes a more "open" posture. These guidelines, however, aren't the Ten Commandments; so none of them is carved in stone. The key to success is finding a comfortable, relaxed position that says, "I care about you and what you are saying."

Leaning

When I'm interested in what people are saying, I naturally tend to lean toward them so they are encouraged to continue speaking.

Leaning too far forward, however, can be inhibiting and very awkward for both parties. If we lean too far into people's

93

personal space, they will usually withdraw and lean away from us. By the same token, moving too far back can send a negative message indicating we'd really rather be someplace else. In America, the ideal distance between two people who are standing or sitting is about the length of one arm. When speaking to a close friend or relative, moving closer is acceptable, of course.

Appropriate Eye Contact

Psalm 139 tells us we are "fearfully and wonderfully made." God gave us a very special channel of silent communication when He created our eyes. In fact, appropriate eye contact is probably the most important ingredient of our SOLAR TEA mixture. In case you're wondering why we don't simply use "eye contact" in our acrostic, it's because appropriateness is so crucial to helping another person feel comfortable and at ease.

There are times when establishing direct eye contact may cause extreme discomfort in a Seeker. When people are overcome with grief or shame, for instance, they will often not want to meet our gaze. But most of the time people appreciate the acute sensitivity that can only be expressed through our eyes. Even at painful moments, it's reassuring to see caring and understanding in the eyes of another.

Of course, we certainly don't want to "stare down" or gaze unblinkingly at others until they feel awkward. Nor do we want to avoid eye contact altogether. In our American culture, appropriate eye contact shows that we're paying attention to the other person. It's an inviting and healthy nonverbal that helps establish warmth. In fact, if we break eye contact too frequently, we may be sending an unintentional message that we don't care what the other person is telling us.

Believe it or not, by breaking eye contact we may even be implying dishonesty. A study by Ohio State sociology lecturer Daniel Quinn found that people tell fewer lies when they look you straight in the eye than when they let their eyes wander.[12] Other research, Quinn reports, has shown that people avoid eye contact while telling a lie. But his study is the first to examine whether eye contact itself affects how much a person lies. Business training seminars have long taught that the best way to establish credibility with a person is to look him directly in the eyes for a minimum of five seconds at a time.[13]

Research has also shown that women tend to use eye contact more than men and are, consequently, generally perceived as much warmer than their male counterparts. Women also seem less inhibited than men in expressing warm caring toward others.

Relaxation

Relaxation and confidence are also important keys to establishing a warm connection with a Seeker. The rule of thumb is to be as relaxed as possible while remaining attentive to the other person. When you notice your body language is not warm, calmly take a deep breath and encourage yourself to relax. I realize telling you to relax after asking you to become more conscious of what your body language is communicating to others sounds a bit contradictory. At first, as you work on increasing your warmth, you'll probably feel a bit self-conscious; but you'll also find that eventually you can become quite comfortable with heightened self-awareness — especially as you see the Seeker relax and go deeper into the conversation.

Touch

Ross Buck, a University of Connecticut professor who studies and writes about personal relations, maintains that the closer to the equator we get, the more hugging people do.[14] He says that no one knows why, but he theorizes that it might have something to do with the day-night cycle. For whatever reason, according to Buck, cultures that encourage caring, non-possessive touch seem to produce healthier, happier people. I guess we shouldn't be surprised. Decades of hospital studies have shown conclusively that cuddling and caressing premature babies increases their survival rate and lowers their overall level of anxiety.

Because the need for caring touch is extremely powerful in human beings, this is an area of extreme sensitivity. In our sexually supercharged culture, touch has taken on meanings that can cause conflict and misunderstanding. Whether the person you're talking with is of the same or the opposite sex, touch can frequently be misinterpreted. Even the most innocent hug, for example, could be interpreted as an aggressive gesture.

Early in a relationship, any touch other than a handshake is usually too threatening and may cause the person to close down or withdraw. As you develop a caring relationship and mutual trust, however, an encouraging pat on the back, a touch on the arm or even a hug may be appropriate. The most effective touch is always gentle and non-possessive.

Since we are not sure how another individual will respond to a touch or a hug, the best thing to do is ask, "Is it O.K. if I give you a hug?" Then listen and watch their nonverbal responses. If the person is comfortable, a brief encouraging hug or touch is often appropriate. If, on the other hand, you sense discomfort, let the person know you will respect his personal boundaries.

It's unfortunate that caring touch is being sexualized, for hugs and other gestures of warmth can, indeed, be therapeutic. Canadian author and therapist Kathleen Keating, for example, calls hugging a "basic need" which, unfortunately, gets distorted in the process of growing up.[15] This is especially true for today's middle-aged Baby Boomers whose parents were products of the parenting styles promoted in the 1950s — styles which were generally strict and devoid of much physical affection.

The family therapist Virginia Satir said that each of us needs four hugs daily to survive, eight to stay emotionally healthy and twelve to grow.[16] Unfortunately, even with numerous studies and respected professionals emphasizing the importance of touch, our jaded 20th century culture often looks with suspicion on any form of caring physical contact. Ironically, it's in this same age of technology, during which we've become so impersonal, that we're hungry for the gentleness and warmth that a simple hug or pat on the back can give.

As Professor Buck explains, all cultures regard touch and hugging as intimate behavior. But each culture regulates the level of intimacy. In a study he conducted, couples were observed at restaurants to see how many times they touched each other. In England, the average was zero per hour; in Gainesville, Florida, 2; in Paris, 110; in Puerto Rico, 180.[17]

We bring out these cultural differences merely to emphasize that, as good communicators and sensitive Helpers, we must be aware of what is accepted and what is not in the particular environment in which we find ourselves. And we must, of course, adapt accordingly.

Environment

Numerous studies have been done on ergonomics — the effective placement of things like chairs, desks and other furniture in a room. Remember, I suggested that the young therapist in training move his chair closer to the couple he was helping. I've also suggested that pastors and those who listen to people in their office regularly rearrange their sofas and desks to create a more inviting "conversation pod" type arrangement.

I sometimes suggest that Helpers remove all physical barriers that separate people and that could detract from warm relationships. Tables, floral arrangements, house plants and knick-knacks, that we've gotten used to, can get in the way of open communication and personal warmth when people have to peer through them to see us.

While I was serving on the staff of a large church with a traditional Presbyterian raised pulpit, we suggested that the sky-high vantage point from which we spoke cut me off from the congregation and created a cold, austere environment for the congregation. After a predictable struggle over church tradition, we removed the old pulpit and began addressing the congregation from a lower level. The change in warmth was sensational. Not only did the services become more lively, people also began to connect more with each other in positive fellowship. In fact, the first thing I hear from people who visit a new church is how "warm" or "cold" it was, and they don't mean in Fahrenheit or Celsius.

Take a moment to look at your home or office environment. How much warmth does it communicate? Does it detract from human warmth? How far away are you forced to sit from each other? Your common sense and "gut feel" will probably be enough to guide you in creating a warmer, more inviting environment.

Accommodating Attitude

An attitude that understands and accepts the differences of others is a must in communicating warmth. In my studies and travels, I've come to realize that every person comes from a slightly different culture and all communication is, therefore, cross-cultural to some extent. Even siblings don't have the same culture or personality. Other people aren't always moved to excitement or frustration by the same things that move me. Things that I find funny often produce anger or apathy in others. Because I find that most people don't think, feel or do things the way I would like, I have to extend a lot of grace to others and receive it from them in return.

One area that we must constantly adjust to if we want to communicate warmth is different energy levels. If the person is very excited and I sit placidly smiling and nodding my head, she could interpret this as disinterest or a patronizing attitude. If, on the other hand, I match the seeker's energy level as much as I can, that person will sense that I care about how she feels. When Scripture exhorts us to mourn with those who mourn and rejoice with those who rejoice, it is encouraging us to extend grace by entering into their frame of reference.

As a therapist, I find many couple conflicts grow out of misunderstandings that arise between mates because each comes from a unique world. Some differences may be male/ female, while others stem from variances in the way each partner was reared. Birth order is another major source of

differences, that requires us to work at accommodating ourselves to others. In some ways, the Politically Correct (PC)
movement is an attempt to sensitize us to these issues. The
problem with PC, however, is that its harsh, legalistic and
punitive approach fosters even more stereotyping and misunderstanding. Only an attitude of love and forgiveness can
break down the racial, cultural and religious barriers that
exist worldwide.

A Process, Not a Program

While we've created an acrostic to emphasize the various
elements that go into human warmth, it's important to
remember that developing these attitudes and skills is not a
program but a process, and like any process, it must be
practiced.

Discomfort at learning a new skill is a natural result of growth
and change because our bodies and minds need time to adjust
and assimilate. Remember what it felt like learning to ride a
bicycle? In fact, I put training wheels on my kids' bikes until
they got the hang of it. The SOLAR TEA acrostic is intended
to give you training wheels through the first stages of learning
how to communicate warmth more effectively. Once you have
learned it well, you can ride with no hands!

Measuring Warmth

When it comes to learning and honing new skills, all of us need
a tool to help us gauge how we're doing. In his research on
effective helping, Robert Carkhuff developed a scale for mea-
suring what he called "facilitative" or therapeutic warmth.[18] If
we think of Carkhuff's scale in terms of a thermometer (or
Warmthometer as I call it), our goal in building a relationship
is 3.0 or "room temperature." Below this level most people feel
uncomfortably cool or cold. On the other hand, unless a
trusting relationship has already been well-established, anything above 3.0 feels too threatening or hot.

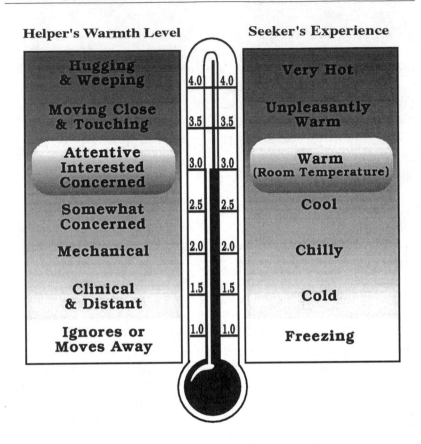

In trying to gauge your warmth, keep in mind that your audience will usually let you know when you're too cold or too warm. Awareness is the first step; self-consciousness follows, and successful change comes from perseverance.

There is tremendous power in warmth.

So, now that you know how to move the mercury on the *Warmthometer*, let's take a look at another critical quality of healthy relationships — empathy.

RADAR Listening

When Julia, 54, talked to her friend Pam, she was at the end of her rope.

A few months prior, Julia's husband of 30 years had died suddenly from a massive coronary attack. In a sincere effort to console her, family, friends and co-workers immediately began to shower her with sympathetic and caring gestures. Widows from the church offered comfort by hovering around her and saying things like, "You must miss him so much" and, "I know just how you feel."

"They don't understand how I feel," Julie blurted out through bitter tears.

Without knowing more about Julia's background, you might not understand her frustration. During her long, unhappy marriage with Bill, she was emotionally and physically abused. She endured the situation, never sharing her secret pain with anyone. But when family and friends began to flock to her with uninformed sympathy, Julia just couldn't take it.

"These people think they know how I feel. They don't!" she told Pam. "I'm not *grieving* over Bill's death. I'm *relieved!* For the first time in 30 years, I feel free to be at home with no fear of abuse!"

This may sound shocking, but mixed in with Julia's feelings of anger, guilt and regret was an understandable sense of liberation from decades of horror. None of Julia's well-meaning family or friends really understood what she was going through because they misinterpreted her true situation and, therefore, her feelings. Julia was grateful for Pam's patient listening because she was the first person who had taken the time to gain a true understanding of what she was thinking and feeling. As a result, Julia felt free to tell Pam the truth about Bill and the truth about what was happening inside her deep heart.

Fortunately for Julia, Pam had learned the skill of reflective listening. Julia's other friends were caring and well-meaning, but couldn't get beyond their own sympathetic reactions to her outward plight.

Julia's story graphically illustrates that sympathy, although a natural response to suffering in others, can often become a subtle barrier to understanding and helping others.

If you are unclear or confused about the difference between sympathy and empathy, let me clarify by telling the story of:

Pete And The Pit

Pete was walking along a country road when he accidentally tumbled into a deep pit which had been camouflaged by fallen leaves and other debris. A very caring and *sympathetic* fellow named Paul (Helper Number One) came along and, seeing that his brother was in trouble, charged forward to help. However, Paul's sympathetic identification with Pete's feelings of fear and anxiety led him to jump into the pit with Pete to make Pete feel better.

The second Helper who came along, Pierre, saw Pete's predicament but took one look at his watch and concluded that there wasn't time to get Pete and Paul out of the pit. So he moved on down the road.

Fortunately, following close behind was Helper Number Three, a genuinely *empathic* individual named Mary, who saw the predicament and recognized that Pete and Paul needed help.

102

She carefully listened to Pete's story, so she could *understand* the situation as accurately as possible. Once Pete and Paul calmed down and explained what had happened, they could begin with Mary's help to think of ways to get out of the pit. Before long Pete suggested that Mary tie a rope to a nearby tree and throw the end down to the bottom of the pit so each of them could climb out.

Neither sympathy (over-identification) nor callousness (under-identification) is biblical. **Empathy**, defined in this book as *communicating accurate understanding*, shows our care and compassion for others and helps them move toward health. Thus, empathy is consistent with biblical love.

The primary method for demonstrating empathy is called active or reflective listening, or what we sometimes refer to as RADAR listening. Although it can be learned as a skill, reflective listening requires an attitude of respect and concern along with the Spirit's fruit of peace, patience and self-control.

Levels of reflective listening correspond to the levels of the upside-down heart discussed in Chapter 6. Foundational listening skills focus on understanding and responding to the open area of the heart as the Seeker shares with us.

As you can tell from Pete's story, the first step in any effective helping process is understanding what the *Seeker* wants and needs from us. Our temptation is often to inappropriately "jump in" with our own answers without fully understanding what the person is seeking. The actual helpfulness of our response depends on how accurately we're able to determine the kind of assistance the Seeker really wants.

What's The Question?

In many instances, people are simply looking for directions or *information*. An effective Helper will make sure she understands exactly what the Seeker is asking for first and then, if possible, offer the requested information. Similarly, if someone asks you to help him fix his car or give him a ride, that person is looking for *action*. The appropriate response is to listen first to make sure you understand the request and then tell him if you are willing to perform the action he is requesting. If the person wants to involve you in gossip or other *inappropriate interactions*, the best response is to affirm the person while declining to participate in the unhealthy activity.

In any case, listening is an essential first step in responding helpfully.

Because there are so many cultural, emotional and language barriers to communication, the skill of empathy is a valuable tool in all circumstances, even when the requests are simple or straightforward.

Once while teaching this skill at a church, I realized that some in the class were skeptical of the practical value of reflective listening until a man in his late thirties spoke up to say that he was the top salesman in a large real estate company and his success lay in having learned to use reflective listening to discover how best to meet the needs of his customers.

Contrary to what you might expect, the greatest cause of problems and conflict in companies, churches and families often isn't disagreement over *answers* to basic questions — but a lack of agreement about what the real *questions* are. This is why the skill of empathy is essential for managers, workers, parents, teachers and pastors. It's also crucial for effective Helpers.

Getting to deep-heart issues requires a combination of peace, self-control, and reflective listening that encourages the Seeker to explore the threatening areas of pain or mystery.

Reflective listening, then, is most important when interacting with people who want:

- To have someone understand them.
- Help in clarifying a problem.
- Involvement and friendship .
- To express deep feelings, such as anger, pain, sadness, confusion, excitement, happiness and joy.

What does the Seeker want from you?

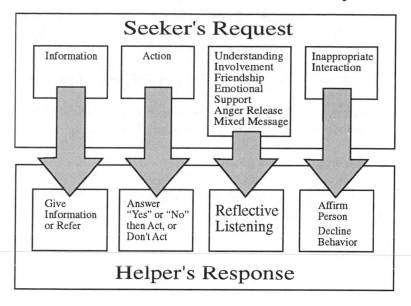

In each of these situations, a person interacting with empathy offers others an opportunity to better explore and understand themselves and their situation. Empathy also provides the necessary foundation to build deeper communication with the person who wants to explore deeper issues. It is, in effect, an invitation to build trust gradually by giving the Seeker full control of the direction the communication takes. A closer look will reveal that showing empathy is a way of offering grace to others. Empathy is patient, kind, and gentle ... It develops the tender fruit of the Spirit in our interaction with others.

On the following page is a practical exercise in assessment, or determining what a Seeker is looking for.

Assessment Exercise

In the following exercise, try to determine what each person is seeking. Fill in the blank to indicate whether the written statement is a request for:

I - Information   **A** - Action   **II** - Inappropriate Interaction

RL - RADAR or Reflective Listening (used when the Seeker has a need for understanding or emotional release)

More than one answer is possible.

1. _I_ Where do we sign up for fall classes?
2. _RL_ Do you know what happened? Your dog ate my best slippers!
3. _II_ Did you hear what she said about Judy's sister?
4. _A_ My car won't start. Do you know anything about fixing cars?
5. _II_ I heard that Bill and Nancy are getting marriage counseling. Do you think they'll get divorced?
6. _RL_ I saw a really interesting show on TV last night. It was about how many people change careers in mid-life.
7. _RL_ Nobody at work cares how I feel. They just want to use me.
8. _I_ I'm feeling sick. Where is the bathroom?
9. _RL_ Ever since last night I've been so mad I could scream.
10. _RL_ Boy, married life is tough. I'm really getting tired and feel like giving up.
11. _A_ I've fallen and I can't get up!
12. _IRL_ What does the Bible say about premarital sex? Is it really wrong?
13. _IRL_ Do you know any good books on coping with depression?
14. _RL_ My children are making me crazy!
15. _II_ We need to pray for Gary, and you'll never guess why. . .

Key: 1) I; 2) RL; 3) RL or II; 4) A; 5) II or RL; 6) RL;
7) RL; 8) I; 9) RL; 10) RL; 11) A; 12) RL;
13) RL; 14) RL; 15) II or RL.

106

This exercise probably revealed just how difficult it can be to exactly categorize another person's comments. Thus, to respond appropriately and accurately is a challenge. In fact, it's one reason we're teaching the listening skills. It's hard to go too far wrong if you employ good listening skills. As a counselor, I've found that these tools are critically important in responding to even the most "simple" interaction. In all my years of using them, they have never let me down.

Reflective RADAR

Effective reflective listening is a critical tool for developing clear communication. Without it we find that we often get confused or end up on a totally different "wavelength" from the Seeker. That's why I like to equate it with RADAR. Like RADAR, it helps me to "locate" or understand where people are coming from and where they're heading.

Think of the high stakes communication between an airline pilot and the airport tower. They're in constant communication. If the folks in the tower are going to provide help to the pilot, they must maintain a clear understanding of the location, speed, altitude and direction of the airplane. The air traffic controllers constantly check their understanding of what the pilot's needs and intentions are. When the pilot gives them information, they often repeat it to verify and insure accurate understanding. They know that lives depend on the quality of their communication.

In our analogy the Seeker is the pilot; the Helper is in the tower. The Seeker controls the steering, the throttle and the altitude. They have the ultimate responsibility for getting to their own destination. The Helper assists and attempts to make the journey as safe as possible.

Reflective or RADAR listening is beneficial in establishing a healthy Helper/Seeker relationship because it:

- Tests Helper's understanding of what Seeker has said.
- Helps the Seeker feel understood.

- Helps the Seeker better understand himself or herself.
- Encourages the Seeker to continue and to go deeper if he wants to.
- Allows for a gentle and safe entry into the deep heart.

Seekers develop a deep sense of trust in a Helper when they feel understood and listened to. The Seeker sets the pace and determines the amount and type of information to share. Given this kind of freedom, Seekers are far more likely to share an open, honest and complete picture of their inner thoughts and feelings. Usually Seekers discover thoughts and feelings they were never consciously aware of before. They gain new and deeper insights into themselves and into new options for changing their lives for the better.

When you find yourself in the role of Helper, keep in mind that your empathic responses provide a "mirror" that reflects the Seeker's inner life back to him. Your empathy and understanding can often provide an effective door-opener for the Holy Spirit to speak to both of you.

RADAR and reflective listening both work by the principle of reflection. We listen intently and carefully to the exact words and thoughts of a person and then check out whether we heard accurately or not by *reflecting* back the essence of the thoughts and feelings in our own words. If we have heard and reflected accurately, they will let us know by saying, "Yes!" or "That's it!" If we miss all or part of their meaning, we will usually be corrected. "No, it's not like that. It's more like. . ."

Most people appreciate our honest attempts to understand them accurately and will work to help us do better. Like RADAR, reflective listening allows us to track the movement of a person's thoughts and feelings.

This corresponds to the green light area of the *teleios* helping model from Chapter 6.

Thoughts and feelings are like coordinates that allow us to zero in on what's happening in another person's heart and mind.

If a friend says, "I'm really excited about being chosen as Parent of the Year by the PTA!" she's helping us understand what's happening inside of her. The feeling coordinate is *excitement*. The thought coordinate is *being chosen as Parent of the Year*.

We might reflect back both the thought and feeling in other words: "You sound really thrilled about this special honor!"

The person usually feels good to know that someone wants to connect with her thoughts and feelings. Sometimes people are even a bit surprised when they hear what they've just said, "I guess I *am* thrilled! And why not? I've put a lot of time and energy into our school."

If they want to examine their thoughts and feelings at a deeper level, the fact that we have communicated accurate understanding encourages them to go on.

Learning RADAR listening

Once we've established that a person is looking for under-standing, involvement, friendship or a chance to express their feelings, there are only three basic steps to formulating an accurate empathic response:

- Identify the *feeling* content that you hear expressed.
- Identify the *thought* content that you hear expressed.
- *Tentatively summarize* or paraphrase what you hear in your own words.

Although RADAR or reflective listening sounds simple, it's not easy. Perhaps because of the influence of Freud, we seem to need to *interpret* what we think people *mean* rather than what they said.

We must be careful not to confuse thoughts with feelings. How many times have you heard someone say, "I feel Mr. Smith is a good instructor"? This statement is not a feeling. It's a thought. You *think* Mr. Smith is a good instructor. This is a judgment you've made about a person, not a feeling. Make sure you're using words that describe actual emotions such as *mad*, *sad*, *glad*, *confused*, *ashamed* or *disgusted*.

Identify Thought vs. Feeling

In the following sentences, identify the thought statements and the feeling statements. Write T or F before each example to identify it as a Thought statement or a Feeling statement. Where *feel* is used incorrectly, mark through it and write in the correct word above it.

__F__ 1. I feel anxious when my 16-year-old drives the car.

__T__ 2. I feel [think] that more men should take this class.

__T__ 3. I feel [think] it's wrong for women to teach men.

__F__ 4. I feel angry when you talk about my mother.

__F__ 5. I feel concerned that you're working too hard.

__F__ 6. I feel scared when I'm home alone.

__T__ 7. I feel [think] my wife needs to change.

__F__ 8. I feel excited when I see how quickly you're learning!

__F__ 9. I feel anxious and excited when I think about traveling.

__T__ 10. I feel [think] that the new pastor is an excellent teacher.

__F__ 11. I feel relieved when I know my children are at home.

__T__ 12. I feel [think] that you are insensitive to the needs of singles.

__T__ 13. I feel [think] that your comments were uncalled for.

__F__ 14. I feel bewildered by your reactions to what I said.

__T__ 15. I feel [think] he's guilty.

Key:

1) F; 2) T; 3) T; 4) F; 5) F; 6) F; 7) T; 8) F; 9) F; 10) T; 11) F; 12) T; 13) T; 14) F; 15) T.

As you can see, people commonly misuse or confuse feelings with beliefs or judgments. If you're very analytical, you may discover that you have some difficulty identifying feeling words. We've included the feeling word list on the last page of this book to help you find the right feeling words when you need them. Most feeling words fall into seven basic emotional states: *mad, sad, glad, afraid, confused, ashamed* and *alone*. The words are grouped according to the depth of the feelings indicated — from a little to a lot.

Remember, in listening to a Seeker's statement we need to focus on the terms that describe emotions as well as the thoughts or beliefs the person is having. Now let's take a short statement and look at it in these terms to see just how simple, yet challenging, it can be.

Seeker statement:

"It really burns me up to have to pay so much in taxes."

Start by identifying the feeling content.

The Seeker feels _angry_.

In the words quoted here, the phrase "burns me up" expresses frustration, anger, or irritation. Any of these feelings would accurately reflect what the Seeker has said.

Next, try to understand why the Seeker has these particular feelings. In other words what are his thoughts?

The Seeker believes _has to pay too much taxes_.

In this case, the Seeker is frustrated because he believes his taxes are too high.

Now try to *tentatively* paraphrase the thought and feeling together without sounding like a parrot or (worse yet) a fugitive from Psychology 101.

You might try one of these:

It sounds like having so much money go to taxes really aggravates you.

You sound pretty steamed up about giving so much money to the government.

It's rather irritating to give up so much of your hard-earned money to the tax man.

A good basic formula for RADAR listening is:

"It sounds like you feel ___angry___ **because** ___taxes are so high___**."**

A tentative response like this indicates that you're trying to understand the Seeker's thoughts and feelings, but you're leaving room for correction. It also leaves the door wide open for more dialogue. During any subsequent interaction, you can adjust your listening responses to match the Seeker's own understanding and insight because he'll usually tell you if you're listening with accurate empathy. Here are a few Seeker statements to help you to learn to construct an appropriate empathic response:

1. *"I can't go to the picnic this weekend. John will be there! I don't think I could stand seeing him with someone else."*

(Feeling) ___anxious___ **(because or about)**
(Thought) ___Seeing John with another woman___

Tentative Paraphrase:

_____

_____

_____

2. *"Whenever I think about the promotion my boss promised me, I start to get all jittery inside."*

(Feeling) _fear excitement_ **(because or about)**

(Thought) _promotion_

Tentative Paraphrase:

Your feeling excited about your promotion?

3. *"I wonder what I've done to make her mad this time? I can't do anything right around here. No matter how hard I try to please her, she just glares at me like I'm some kind of jerk."*

(Feeling) _anger_ **(because or about)**

(Thought) _the way she responds to him_

Tentative Paraphrase:

You're irritated about the way she treats you?

4. *"Since I quit smoking I haven't been able to relax. I can't concentrate. I'm irritable all the time. I eat like a walrus. I'm not sure I can survive without my cigarettes."*

(Feeling) _____ **(because or about)**

(Thought) _____

Tentative Paraphrase:

You're not tolerating not smoking?

There are many possible responses to each of the statements above. If you found that you needed to think hard before responding, that's because it takes real effort to accurately reflect what another is feeling and thinking. Did you find it more difficult to identify the thought or the feeling?

Because of our temperament or personality preferences, some of us naturally focus on the feeling part of a statement while others tend to hear only the thinking part. In fact, some researchers think that there is a 50/50 split on thinking/ feeling orientation. This is also true for those who are sharing: some folks use feeling words and feeling statements, while others stick to thoughts.

Empathy teaches all of us the value of balance in our communication. As the chart below illustrates, *accurate* empathy depends on hearing both the emotional state and the cognitive state of a Seeker.

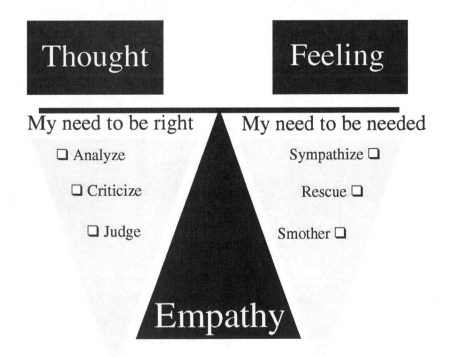

Thought Feeling

My need to be right My need to be needed

❏ Analyze Sympathize ❏

❏ Criticize Rescue ❏

❏ Judge Smother ❏

Empathy

Balancing thought and feeling responses is essential in over-coming the barriers of under-identification and over-identification discussed in Chapter 4. By overemphasizing the thought content of what another says, we quickly become detached analysts of the person's situation rather than caring friends and helpers. Also, by remaining aloof from Seeker feelings, our helping rapidly degenerates into analysis, criticism and judgmentalism.

It's equally damaging to focus exclusively on feeling content. When we do so, we face temptation to over-identify with the Seeker's feelings and become caught up in sympathy, rescuing and emotional smothering instead of facilitating growth. Those of us who are already prone to codependent over-functioning are especially vulnerable in this department.

Using RADAR listening effectively requires both balance and accuracy. Our goal here is communicating real understanding of what Seekers are telling us — not interpreting or correcting them.

One time while I was teaching a group of senior managers on the importance of clear communication, the president of the company stood up and began to pace while talking about the pressure his industry was experiencing because of the current economic slowdown. After several minutes, he paused and I attempted to summarize his thoughts and feelings to see if my human RADAR machine was tracking accurately. My reflective statement went something like this: "It sounds as though the financial cutbacks are really causing you some anxiety. I wonder if. . ."

At this point he interrupted me and said, "I'm not anxious. This is a great opportunity for our company!"

As a Helper/consultant, I missed the mark by using a *loaded* emotional term that the president *had not stated.* My over-stating his emotional language blocked communication, so I backed up, apologized and tried again with words like "challenge," "pressure" and "stress." His reaction this time was much more positive.

Like much else pertaining to human relationships, effective empathy is more of an art and a skill than an exact science. Our *Empathometer* illustrates that our basic goal, just as in *warmth*, is the 3.0 level where our listening responses are interchangeable with what the Seeker has said.

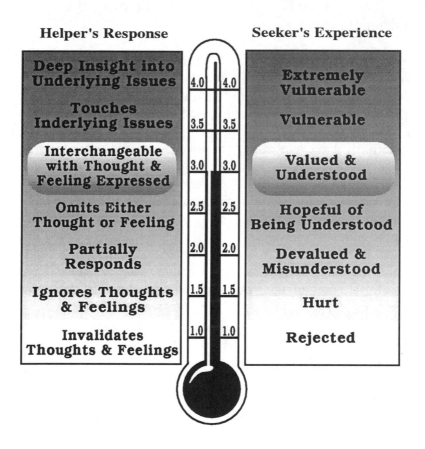

Helper's Response			Seeker's Experience
Deep Insight into Underlying Issues	4.0	4.0	Extremely Vulnerable
Touches Inderlying Issues	3.5	3.5	Vulnerable
Interchangeable with Thought & Feeling Expressed	3.0	3.0	Valued & Understood
Omits Either Thought or Feeling	2.5	2.5	Hopeful of Being Understood
Partially Responds	2.0	2.0	Devalued & Misunderstood
Ignores Thoughts & Feelings	1.5	1.5	Hurt
Invalidates Thoughts & Feelings	1.0	1.0	Rejected

Developing and using effective empathy takes practice — and lots of it. Many studies have determined that, generally speaking, it takes about 30 days of practice to change a behavior. So don't worry if you feel uncomfortable with your empathy skills at first, especially if this is a new concept to you.

Being Tentative

Keep in mind that empathy assists Seeker self-exploration. In learning to listen reflectively, we must remember to be *tentative* in our lead statements with another. This re-emphasizes that we're in a discovery process with the Seeker. In other words, since it's impossible to know exactly what's happening inside another person's mind and heart, we need to learn how to respond provisionally. This not only prevents our coming across as a know-it-all, but it also leaves the responsibility for the decision of "Yes, that's what I said" to the Seeker.

We communicate an open attitude through our voice tone and nonverbals, as well as through words. For example, ending our statement with the inflection of a question: "So you're saying you feel confused by your daughter's need for a hug one moment and her rejection of your affection the next?"

Even when we're pretty sure we've correctly perceived what someone else is telling us, we're usually better received when we're tentative. We want to communicate genuine understanding and concern — not the impression that we're omniscient. We can help put Seekers at ease and develop healthier, more helpful relationships by starting to assume that they're the best authorities on their thinking and feeling processes. Here are some suggestions for tentative openings:

- *I wonder if. . .*
- *I'm not sure I'm following you, but. . .*
- *I think I heard you say. . .*
- *Am I hearing you say. . .*
- *Correct me if I'm wrong, but. . .*
- *Is it possible that. . .*
- *You seem to be saying. . .*
- *Perhaps you're saying. . .*
- *I sense that you're feeling. . .*
- *I wonder if you're feeling. . .*
- *Sounds like. . .*
- *Do I hear you saying. . .*

You get the general idea.

Even when you're confident that you've correctly perceived your Seeker's thoughts and feelings, it's still helpful to form your response in a tentative manner with openers like these:

- *It sounds as though you feel. . .*
- *From your point of view. . .*
- *In your experience. . .*
- *I hear you saying that. . .*

These gentle leads serve a number of helpful purposes. In addition to putting a person at ease, they allow you to respond to the words of the person rather than forcing you to come up with answers. Being tentative with people allows them to come to their own conclusions.

Seeker: *I've had about all I can take from my boss! If she doesn't ease off the pressure, I'm getting out.*

Helper: *Wow! It sounds like you're irritated enough with your boss to even consider [tentatively] leaving your job.*

Seeker: *No, I can't afford to quit right now, but I sure feel like it lately.*

In the interaction above, the Seeker was able to clarify without feeling awkward about contradicting the Helper. In the example below, you can see how different and challenging and counterproductive a non-tentative response can be:

Helper: *You're going to quit your job ! Boy, you must be really mad.*

Seeker: *I didn't say that I was going to quit my job.*

Helper: *Yes, you did.*

Avoid Asking Questions

In general, effective empathy avoids *direct questions* and relies, instead, on listening to the words and watching for nonverbals the Seeker uses. Especially in the initial phases of helping, we want the Seeker to set the pace and direction. The goal of empathic listening is to encourage people to explore their own inner lives. If we take control of the conversation away from the person by asking direct questions, it usually becomes threatening and counterproductive. Directive questions may help us satisfy our curiosity or assert our own pace and agenda, but empathic listening is more effective in helping Seekers get below a surface level of self-awareness and move on to healthy action steps.

Direct questions also tend to engender defensive resistance. Ever since children began to be put on the spot at school by big, powerful teachers, humans have tried to avoid the glare of pointed questions. Therefore, effective Helpers learn to avoid any interaction that results in a Seeker withdrawing in fear.

Questions may be quite appropriate later in the helping process as the Seeker begins to concretely examine new insights and ideas. This is the concreteness stage of the *teleios* model as is taught in the second course of this series. There you will learn specific ways to ask key questions.

If you remember the traffic light discussed in the earlier chapters, you will realize that concreteness belongs in the more threatening yellow light phase. Although it's only human to want to move on quickly to action, the *teleios* "Grace Based Model" encourages patience and self-control so that Seekers can safely choose life in their own time frame.

Remember the Adverse Advisors from Chapter 5? It's often tempting and always easier to offer clichés instead of empathy. Perhaps you can identify some of the Adverse Advisors who would say things such as:

- *I know just how you feel. . .*
- *Let me tell you what happened to me. . .*
- *You think that's bad! Did you hear. . .*
- *You're feeling that way because. . .*
- *You better not think that way. . .*
- *You better not feel that way. . .*
- *Listen, I know what you should do. . .*

119

- *I'm sure that everything will be all right. . .*
- *Just hang in there. . .*
- *Now, don't be upset. . .*
- *You're in a heap of trouble. . .*
- *Well, praise the Lord anyway!*

Reflect a moment on a recent conversation where the person interacted with superficial clichés rather than really hearing you out. Did you like the way it felt, or would you prefer an empathic interaction?

Scripture and research agree on the value of caring and listening. James 1:19 exhorts us: "Everyone should be quick to listen, slow to speak and slow to become angry . . ." Proverbs is also pointed in its admonition to avoid giving advice at the expense of listening: "A fool finds no pleasure in understanding but delights in airing his own opinions . . . He who answers before listening — that is his folly and his shame" (Proverbs 18:2,13).

On the other hand: "Pleasant words are a honeycomb, sweet to the soul and healing to the bones" (Proverbs 16:24).

Volumes of information have been released within the last few years with research focusing on the positive and life changing effects of effective listening at home, at school and in the workplace. Empathy has been shown to be a necessary component of moral behavior, to be a foundation for stronger, healthier relationships. Medical schools have seen the cost benefits of empathy. Studies indicate that, if doctors will use as little as 45 seconds of empathy with a patient, they are far less likely to be sued for malpractice.

There are many good reasons to do it, but why is it so hard?

You May Sweat A Lot

Developing empathic listening skills feels unnatural for most of us at first. These new ways of listening rub against our ingrained habit patterns. While teaching these skills to a class of Scandinavians, Dave Ping discovered an analogy that may prove helpful for all of us who struggle with applying new skills. Dave, who had never skied a day in his life, awkwardly waddled into a classroom wearing a pair of cross-country skis. "I've never skied before," he told the group of amused Norwegians, Swedes and Danes. "I'm going to give cross-country skiing a try today. Tell me what I can expect when I get out on the snow."

To many Scandinavians cross-country skiing is second nature. So when Dave asked, "What can I expect out there?" their answers were varied but to the point:

- *It will feel quite embarrassing and awkward at first.*

- *You'll be tempted to compare yourself with others who are more experienced.*

- *You will discover muscles you never knew that you had.*

- *It's a lot harder than it looks, but you can do it.*

- *If you give it a chance, you'll soon find you are enjoying yourself.*

- *If you stay away from the big hills at first, you will do just fine.*

- *You'll sweat a lot.*

Of course the same can be said of learning empathic listening. Like any new skill, it will indeed feel awkward and embarrassing at first. It will take lots of effort and practice. But soon, with hard work and God's help, you could find yourself applying the skills with the seemingly effortless grace of an experienced Nordic skier. But stay away from the big hills. You aren't ready to treat depression yet.

As we move down the trail to healthy living and vibrant relationships, we also move naturally into our next phase of our model — communicating respect.

121

R-E-S-P-E-C-T

Who can hear the word respect without thinking of Aretha Franklin belting out the memorable words of her Motown classic: "R-E-S-P-E-C-T. Find out what it means to me!"

Even if you're not familiar with the song itself, the notion that respect often has highly individual meanings is probably no surprise to you. When speaking to groups around the globe, I've heard a variety of interpretations of this simple seven-letter word — many of which are confused and contradictory.

Perhaps the most widespread belief about respect is that it must be *earned*. In this view, respect is a reward we need bestow only upon those whose external accomplishments or successes prove special worthiness. In other words, worth comes from works. Society, in fact, commonly determines a person's *respectability* based on several factors including conduct, physical appearance, social standing, wealth, political views and religious orthodoxy. Those who don't measure up, for whatever reason, are often shunned, discriminated against and generally excluded from polite society.

For more than 16 years, I wore a beard and experienced the prejudice that comes from having an easily observable outward identity. During this time, in the late 60s, many of the students with whom I worked at the university offered me instant respect based on little more than the fact that, to them, I looked trustworthy. One young drug addict came to me for counseling soon after I grew the beard and said that his trust and respect for me changed when I no longer had a smooth face.

At the other extreme were people who lost respect for me when my razor fell silent. Some of the names and stereotypes I was called included *Communist, Quaker, rebel, freak* and *radical.* In fact, some members of my family were concerned about my relationship to God and assumed that I had become a *liberal.*

As a matter of fact, the reddish-brown beard symbolized an outward response to an inward change. Emotionally, spiritually and relationally I had moved more toward a biblical spirituality that resulted in more trust of God, ministry to the poor, focus on family life and stronger stands on issues that my father agreed with. But I didn't *look* like a person who was a conservative, Bible-believing family man getting a doctorate in education. I was being offered respect or lack of respect for the way I looked rather than for who I was.

This kind of discrimination or *partiality* is precisely the opposite of biblical respect.

When 1 Peter 2:17 commands Christians to treat everyone with respect, nobody is excluded. Scripture clearly tells us that God does not show favoritism (Romans 2:11). As we've discussed in earlier chapters, God's assessment of human worth does *not* depend on anything we do. It has nothing to do with who our parents are, what neighborhood we grew up in, how much of our time or money we give to good causes, how smart we are or how spiritual we are. Like God's love for us, His respect is also unconditional. It can't be earned because it's based on our innate God-given *worth* as a person rather than our *work* as persons. A popular phrase says it all: We are human *beings*, not human *doings*.

Respect, which means *communicating value or worth,* could be called the oxygen of human interaction; without it our relationships suffocate and die. As human beings, we were created in such a way that we not only *desire* respect, we *need* it — both to be healthy ourselves and to have healthy relationships with others. Although warmth and empathy are critically important to health, without respect they can degenerate into manipulation and superficiality.

I remember working with a teen-ager with a severe drinking problem. He desperately needed help to overcome his addiction. After six months of hard work and trust building, I finally encouraged him and his family to seek treatment through a hospital program (this was before we established the Life Way Program). I was deeply discouraged by the disrespectful attitude of some of the hospital staff. During the intake procedure, the family was asked to fill out the usual mountain of paperwork. When they hesitated and reluctantly admitted that they were illiterate, the "professional" interviewer laughed at them.

Imagine the devastating effect on that family. Months of trust, progress and hard work almost came to nothing as an offhand and insensitive comment by a condescending clerk nearly robbed this struggling family of the hope they needed to find health for themselves and their child.

Comedian Rodney Dangerfield expresses what many of us feel. "I get no respect!" Dangerfield laments. He brings up situation after situation where he has been belittled or discounted. Although he often exaggerates to the point of absurdity, his humor depends on the fact that most people can identify at some level with his being disrespected and put down.

Teasing/Put-Downs

In the section on theology, we gave a brief overview on the issues of shame and self-esteem, pointing out that low self-esteem is a direct result of the destructiveness of the Fall. Although there is a direct relationship between the work of Christ on the cross and redeemed esteem through adoption, there are also key dimensions of shame and self-esteem that are related to our relationships. Since shame is the personal sense of lost identity and lost inheritance, any behavior that attacks our personhood or inheritance as a child of God reinforces shame and detracts from human esteem.

There is a powerful story for what happens to our esteem when we've been rejected or had our intelligence or character attacked. It tells how each of us was born with an invisible disc hanging around our neck. The disc is called the IALAC (I Am Lovable And Capable).

Whenever we encounter others who treat us with respect, the IALAC grows. But as we encounter toxic tongues, the IALAC is chipped away, reduced in size. If we grow up in families and schools that treat us as God's children who have innate worth, then it's likely that the IALAC will grow large and healthy. But traumatic, disrespectful interactions have the opposite effect, leaving us with IANLAC (I Am *Not* Lovable And Capable).

Why is it that we seem to need to look down on others and elevate ourselves? We've all experienced this urge. Perhaps it's just part of being a fallen person, but the effects can be extremely damaging. As a counselor, I can't count the number of distressed, depressed and angry people who have recounted horror stories about being teased or ridiculed as children. People often experience the effects and hurt long after the event.

I visited recently with an 83-year-old friend, who had grown up with an undiagnosed learning disability. He told me how deeply he had been hurt by his father's disrespectful remarks to him as a child. Many times as they worked on projects or homework together, the father would break off the relationship in anger. My friend still remembered the intense pain and shame that he felt when, 75 years earlier, his dad had called him "Stupid" and "Dummy."

Although he had never shared these memories and feelings before, they were as fresh and painful to him at 83 as they were when he was a boy, perhaps worse, because they festered and grew over the years into what Scripture calls "a root of bitterness" (Hebrews 12:15). As Proverbs 18:21 says, "Death and life are in the power of the tongue" (KJV).

Interestingly, there has actually been research showing that this proverb is true. Psychologist Rich Walters wanted to find out how the words we use impact the physical and emotional health of those to whom we speak. So he hooked people up to a pupilometer, a machine that measures the involuntary response of the listeners' pupils when they hear taped statements of people reading a script.

The results were instructive. When students heard a statement that was cold, non-empathic and/or disrespectful, the involuntary response of their pupils was immediate and in accordance to what they were hearing. They got smaller, indicating a perceived threat. But warm, caring and respectful statements had the opposite effect. The pupils opened up. The way we relate to one another has a definite effect on us physiologically.

Although the strength of our own self-esteem can moderate the pain, toxic tongues of others do cause an immediate wounding of the body, mind and spirit. In *Rational Christian Thinking*[1] and *Breaking Free From the Past*,[2] we teach those wounded by this kind of disrespect how to be healed. Cleaning out the toxins and healing our hurting hearts is necessary when we've been wounded by death-dealing relationships. The purpose of this book is to prevent interpersonal death and to teach skills that minister life.

Jesus confronted this issue in a clear, straightforward manner; and the words He used leave no doubt about His view of the matter. In Matthew 5:21, 22, we hear the ringing words:

> *You have heard that it was said to the people long ago, "Do not murder, and anyone who murders will be subject to judgment." But I tell you that anyone who is angry with his brother will be subject to judgment. Again, anyone who says to his brother, "Raca," is answerable to the Sanhedrin. But anyone who says, "You fool!" will be in danger of the fire of hell.*

There are three levels of harmfulness communicated in this teaching. First, anger alone can lead to judgment, so we need to take care lest we carry around bitterness toward others. Second, *raca*, an attack on another person's intelligence, can lead to being taken before the supreme court for judgment because the pain it causes is much greater than simply holding anger toward a person. Finally, calling a person a fool attacks his character and is deserving of hell. Character assassination or attacking one's self-respect is the most horrible thing that one can do. It's so disturbing that Jesus says it can lead to hellish consequences. In other words, Jesus is saying in metaphorical language the same thing that Dr. Walters discovered in his research. There are various levels of trauma or pain (death) that can be communicated in interpersonal relationships. Jesus is so convinced of this that He warns strongly of the personal dangers of traumatizing others. In fact, if we attack the character of another person we face the worst possible consequences.

Matthew 25:40 makes it clear how highly Jesus values even those whom society considers unworthy of positive regard or respect. He told the disciples, "I tell you the truth, whatever you did for one of the least of these brothers of mine, you did for me." The meaning behind these words gives us a compelling reason to respect others regardless of their conduct or social status. Although we may find it difficult to see beyond the faults, offensive behavior or shortcomings of others, we're encouraged to extend to them the same respect we crave for ourselves.

Christian author C.S. Lewis describes Christian respect in his essay *The Weight of Glory*:

> *There are no ordinary people. . . It is immortals whom we joke with, work with, marry, snub, and exploit—immortal horrors or everlasting splendors. This does not mean we are to be perpetually solemn. We must play. But our merriment must be of that kind . . . which exists between people who have from the onset taken each other seriously — no flippancy, no superiority, no presumption. And your charity must be real and costly love, with deep feelings for the sins in spite of which we love the sinner — no mere tolerance. . . which parodies love. . . Next to the Blessed Sacrament itself, your neighbor is the holiest object presented to your senses.[3]*

For the purposes of this text, we'll define respect as *recognizing and communicating value or unconditional worth.*

The medical and psychological communities have also begun to acknowledge the importance of communicating respect. Both Carl Rogers and Robert Carkhuff[4] not only saw respect or "unconditional high regard" as a basic human need, they also viewed it as an "essential core condition" of helping.

In fact, many experts confirm what common sense would seem to indicate: respect is an indispensable foundation for caring relationships. When respect is clearly communicated to individuals seeking help, it allows them to feel secure in sharing their inner thoughts and feelings without fear of being openly or secretly judged. Research has confirmed the therapeutic value of respect in all kinds of relationships.

- Researcher Frances Klagsburn found that an overwhelming majority of couples married 15 years or longer identify mutual respect as a key factor in the survival and success of their marriages. Her research is echoed by many others who have discovered that respect is crucial to the durability and health of marriages.[5]

- Author Julius Segal suggests that treating our children with the same respect that we would show to adults builds positive self-esteem and enhances discipline. By accepting children for who they are and recognizing their talents along with their developmental limitations, parents will be able to encourage healthy self-responsibility and self-respect.[6]

- According to a study published in the *Personality and Social Psychology Bulletin*, people who have little respect for themselves tend to be more prejudiced. When we judge ourselves harshly without extending grace, we will usually assess racial and social differences negatively as well.[7]

- John Braid writes that developing respectful attitudes and behaviors in employees through systematic training is critical to the success of today's businesses. In an increasingly competitive commercial environment, companies not addressing respect and customer satisfaction will be left behind.[8]

Benefits of Respect

Think about how **you** respond to being treated with respect. When you know that you are valued and accepted for who you are, it's empowering. Even a person with very low self-esteem can discover hope when they are treated with respect. Years of working with inner-city youth and families has shown me (Dave) that demonstrating high levels of positive regard pays off. The more we treat individuals like they are capable of change and are responsible for their actions, the more likely they are to embrace positive growth. When we think that people trust us and believe in us, we not only gain self-esteem, but we are also motivated and energized to live up to their faith in us.

R-E-S-P-E-C-T. Find Out What It Means To Me!

To find out what respect can mean to you in terms of improved relationships, you need look no farther than the word itself. The following acrostic will give you some practical assistance in expressing biblical respect in all your relationships:

Resist using pat answers or manipulation. Simplistic advice-giving or "quick and dirty" problem solving reflect disregard of the seriousness of another's situation. It's insulting and demoralizing when people try to solve our problems with a quick fix or a formula response. A respectful attitude empowers others by encouraging them to explore, understand and solve their own issues.

Rather than attempting to promote your own hidden agenda for change through verbal manipulation, simply listen whole-heartedly to what the Seeker is saying. Nothing raises respect barriers faster than trying to impose our own values or belief systems on another . In doing so, we communicate the idea that the other person's beliefs are not worthy or valuable.

Respect recognizes everyone's God-given ability and responsibility to *choose life* for themselves.

Exercise personal self-responsibility, as opposed to "owning" another person's situations or problems. We believe that the problem ownership aspect of respect is so important that we will devote all of Chapter 10 to explaining it more completely. The unhealthy attitude of taking over ownership of another person's problems communicates the idea that the Seeker is not capable of making good decisions for himself. Rather, when we show respect, we become a paraclete, coming alongside him where he is instead of attempting to push or pull him down the path that we think is best. In doing so, we *cooperate* with the Seeker as he attempts to resolve issues and concerns. Effective helping uses cooperation, not coercion, to bring change.

Suspend all critical judgments and conclusions about the Seeker. As pointed out in Chapter 4, we must constantly be aware of social, educational and racial prejudices (all part of the baggage we bring with us from our varied life experiences). In communicating respect, we concentrate on extending grace to the Seeker — opening our ears, minds and hearts and listening without judgment.

Pray and practice. Respect appears to be a simple concept, but the challenge comes in applying it. That's why we all need prayer and practice. We need to develop a genuine interest in individuals. For most people this does not come naturally. Remember what my pastor friend said, "The only thing that comes naturally is sin: everything else takes work and God's power." When we seek God's help and make an honest effort to respect and care for others, we can embrace 1 Peter 4:8 which tells us to "love each other deeply, because love covers over a multitude of sins."

Extend yourself appropriately. Apply that all-important balance principle: keep things in perspective. Be honest about your limitations — about your own time restraints, availability and needs. We all have the same amount of time, 168 hours in a week. Whether we can admit it to ourselves or not, we have only limited time for helping others. We all have to make difficult choices to keep our lives in balance. While it's tempting to overextend and easy to make promises we can't keep, respect for others requires honesty. Most people can tell when you are unable to give them your complete attention because you're overextended. It's far more helpful to clarify how much time you can realistically give.

It's also important to clarify your moral, ethical and Scriptural limits and boundaries as needed. There are times when you will be either uncomfortable or unqualified to help.

Consider confidentiality. Certainly, without a spirit of trust and confidentiality, there is no respect. What a Seeker shares with us in confidence is privileged information. It belongs within the boundaries of our Helper/Seeker relationship. Christians must be careful not to violate confidentiality through "holy gossip." Perhaps you've witnessed a conversation like this: "Gary, you'll never guess who needs our prayers. . .and why!" Nothing can destroy trust more quickly and thoroughly than such spiritualized scandal-mongering.

There are, of course, limits to confidentiality. When a Seeker shares information that leads you to conclude that the person is a sure and present threat to herself or others, it's necessary to contact the appropriate individuals. Although this is very difficult, it can often prevent unnecessary tragedy. Other situations that might require such action include child or spouse abuse.

Take Seeker comments seriously. Even though it's often easy for us to dismiss some of the comments and remarks of others (usually because of the prejudged ideas and notions we carry around with us), it's paramount that we listen carefully and take seriously the comments and remarks of the Seeker. Oftentimes people will joke or use sarcastic remarks when they're afraid or ashamed to talk directly about a painful issue. Respect dictates that we try not to avoid or cover up any subject that the Seeker brings to us.

As with warmth and empathy, we've developed a scale to help us measure respect. In this case our goal is 3.0 and above.

At the lowest levels of respect, the Helper reveals open contempt for the Seeker's thoughts and feelings. Most of us experience this level of disrespect as attack and respond by either withdrawing or fighting back. Our goal in respect is to approach Seekers with biblical humility – treating them as equals created in the image of God.

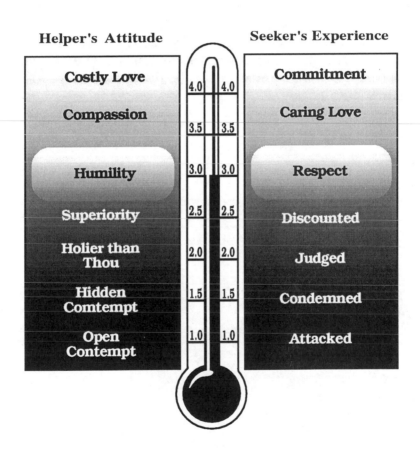

Helper's Attitude		Seeker's Experience
Costly Love	4.0 4.0	Commitment
Compassion	3.5 3.5	Caring Love
Humility	3.0 3.0	Respect
Superiority	2.5 2.5	Discounted
Holier than Thou	2.0 2.0	Judged
Hidden Comtempt	1.5 1.5	Condemned
Open Contempt	1.0 1.0	Attacked

The higher levels of respect require sacrifice on the part of the Helper. Compassion and tough love (honest love that risks rejection) go "the extra mile" in extending grace to our Seeker.

133

If we remember that we are in the same process as our Seekers, it will help us to be more sensitive and respectful toward them. Keep in mind that:

God formed us,
Sin deformed us,
Christ transformed us.
The Holy Spirit is reforming us.

R-E-S-P-E-C-T. Like Aretha and so many others who have discovered the power of respect, we can find out what it means to us and those whose lives we touch. But first, we need to get rid of some *monkeys*. . .

Monkeying Around

Back a number of years ago when my children were little and I was in the start-up phase of our ministry, I learned an important lesson about taking responsibility for myself and not for others.

I've been blessed with a wise and loving wife who not only understands and supports me, but also helps get me back on track when I wander off on a tangent. It happened that one night in particular I had promised to stay home with Karen and the children for some family time, but I got off track.

Predictably, as we sat down to dinner, the phone rang. It was a young woman whom I had been counseling at the Teleios Center. (I don't know how they do it, but some needy people always seem to know when you're about to sit down to dinner.) She had an appointment scheduled with me for the next morning, but she just couldn't wait. She *had* to see me immediately. Right now!

I also reacted predictably. Here was a human being who needed me. She was depending on **me**. I **had** to help her! After all, helping people was what I was called to do. I must also confess that being asked to rescue others always gives me an ego boost and an adrenaline rush like nothing else!

As I talked on the phone, Karen saw that "rescuer's glint" in my eye and sensed what was about to happen. Aware that our rare and valuable family time was about to be sacrificed to another one of my heroic rescue attempts, Karen eased up behind me while I was still on the phone and whispered, "Gary, do you want me to saddle your white horse for you?"

Still driven by a sense of urgency, I shot Karen an irritated look and tried to ignore her message, even though it was a well aimed shot. After a few more minutes, she whispered again in a gleeful tone, "Gary, Gary! You had better hurry up. I hear that horse whinnying down in the basement. I'll go put the saddle on."

This time Karen finally got her message across. It wasn't the caller's need I was responding to at all, but my own need to be a hero. Knowing that, in reality, the caller's situation could wait until morning, I reined in my white steed and gently, but firmly, told the caller that we would discuss her "problem" at our designated appointment time the next day.

This little incident has been a turning point for me. I realized that I had been so caught up in my compulsion to rush in and solve the problems of others that I was ignoring my responsibilities as a husband and father. Karen, God bless her, helped me to admit my addiction to rescuing people and to comprehend the high cost my family was paying to support my habit. It's been a constant battle for 25 years.

Of Monkeys And Men (And Women)

Perhaps you've heard the expression, "He has a monkey on his back." It's a phrase frequently used to refer to a drug addict's habit. In my case the *monkeys* on my back came from an addiction to assume responsibility that didn't belong to me. Now I realize that when I accept anxiety for problems that are clearly not mine and try to solve them, I'm carrying other people's monkeys.

So what is a monkey?

Whenever I do for others things that they are called to do for themselves, I'm placing their monkey on my back. Any time

136

an issue, problem or situation creates anxiety, stress or discomfort in me, it can become a monkey. When I emotionally or physically rescue others or allow them to transfer their personal responsibility for problem-solving to me, I'm taking on the monkey that really belongs to them. And let me tell you, monkeys can be incredibly demanding and nasty little creatures; and some are as big as gorillas!

When a friend, family member or co-worker gives you custody of her monkey, watch out! You may be walking into a no-win situation. No matter how diligently you try to feed, groom, and tend to her monkey, the result usually falls short of the person's demands. In all probability, you'll end up tense, exhausted, irritable and exasperated, while the person you're trying to help feels resentment instead of gratefulness. As a pastor said last week, "Why do people get angry with me when I'm trying so hard to help them?" People seem to intuitively understand that when we take their monkeys, it's disrespectful. As a matter of fact, stress and burnout result not so much from hard work as from carrying monkeys that don't belong to us.

I realize now that when I inappropriately take ownership of other people's problems, I'm not really doing them a favor. By doing for them what they're capable of and need to be doing for themselves, I often rob them of the opportunity to grow and experience greater wholeness or *teleios* for themselves. Instead of helping them toward maturity, I'm really helping them to stay sick. Sometimes I'm actually setting myself up as a savior in their eyes and preventing them from receiving the kind of help they can get only from the true Savior, Jesus Christ.

An article in a 1973 *Harvard Business Review*[1] tells how taking others' monkeys can paralyze even the best managers and business leaders. In fact, it's often the most successful people among us who become "zoo keepers" of others' monkeys. Successful people find success because they are task-oriented problem-solvers. That can, however, be detrimental if I do for others what they could do for themselves.

Irresponsible or dependently immature folks are often drawn to these overfunctioning problem solvers and vice versa. It's a great fit. Neither can succeed without the other. A dependent underachiever must find an overachieving person to do his work, and an overachiever must find someone who will allow the overachiever to do for him what a mature person would do for himself. Pastors, managers, parents and volunteers often find themselves besieged by immature underachievers looking for someone upon whom they can foist their monkeys. The result is burnout.

Being tired out can be solved by getting rest. It's like being out of gas. All you need is some rest and refreshment to fill up the tank. But being burned out comes from running on a lack of oil. The engine gets burned out.

Quadruple Type A Behavior

A prescription for monkey burnout:

A – Anxiety is essential to monkey business and to burn-out. Being more concerned about others' problems than they are is a sure-fire way to go down in flames.

A – Answer experts take responsibility for all healing (omnipotent), all teaching and all correction (omniscient).

A – Always available (omnipresent) is what monkey handlers must be to deal with all of the demands they have heaped on themselves.

A – Angry is often how we feel when things don't work out. This leads to guilt feelings and, thus, to more anxiety. Then you can start the cycle all over again.

Learning to "hear" our inner anxiety, anger and other emotions is one of the three key areas of *Listening for heaven's sake*.

You may look at these "Quadruple Type A" activities and smile because you know someone who's caught in that cycle of despair and burnout. The temptation to be *Answer Expert* (omniscient) is one which I constantly struggle to resist. I never intentionally set out to be omnipotent or omnipresent, but I somehow get caught up in attempting to meet everybody's needs and be everywhere at the same time .

While working as Associate Dean at the University of Cincinnati, I was also leading a house church and working on a doctorate in counseling. There was no question about the fact that I was a busy man, having a wife and two small children as well. After hearing a talk on ministry to the poor, I was overcome with *anxiety* and thoughts of failure which led me to consider ways I could go into the inner city with the *answers* that only *I* could offer. Although my time was extremely limited, there was a sense in which I felt a *compulsion* to be with the poor as well. Although the thoughts were racing furiously around my head, the Lord was able to get through in that still small voice. The dialogue went something like this:

"Gary, are you doing what I've told you to do?"

"Yes, Lord, I am."

"Have I told you to go into the inner city to help the poor?"

"No, Lord, You have not."

"Well, stop trying to be the Messiah. I sent one Messiah, and that's enough. I don't need another one."

Rx for Recovery of Serenity

Rx – **Relinquish** yourself, the Seeker and the Seeker's issues to God. Only He is omnipotent, omniscient and omnipresent.

Rx – **Receive** the Word of God. Hear God's directions about what to do. (We will discuss listening to God in greater depth in the next chapter.) Then *respond* by doing the *right* thing.

Rx – **Relax.** "Be still (relax) and know that I am God."

Covenant of Relinquishment

I do solemnly swear that I will:

1. Relinquish to God all my claims to run the universe.
2. Relinquish to God all of my desires and temptations to be omnipresent, omniscient and omnipotent.
3. Relinquish to God all desires and schemes to save others (including my family).
4. Relinquish to God my desire to work 169 hours per week.

Signed _____ Date _____

Witnessed By _____

Sharing Burdens And Carrying Loads

"But wait a minute," you may say. "Doesn't Scripture tell us to 'bear one another's burdens'?"

What's the difference between carrying monkeys and bearing burdens? A close examination of Galatians 6:1-5 provides the answers.

> *Brothers, if someone is caught in a sin, you who are spiritual should restore him gently. But watch yourself, or you also may be tempted. Carry each other's **burdens**, and in this way you will fulfill the law of Christ.*
>
> *If anyone thinks he is something when he is nothing, he deceives himself. Each one should test his own actions. Then he can take pride in himself, without comparing himself to somebody else, for each one should carry his own **load**.*

When we read these verses in context, they provide us with a seeming paradox. In verse 2 we are, indeed, told to carry each other's *burdens;* but in verse 5, we're told that each person must carry his own load. This sounds contradictory, but the distinction is very clear in the original Greek text.

140

The Greek word for burden is *baros*. It means something heavy pressing down on a person physically, emotionally and/or spiritually. The concept here is a weight too big to be carried alone.

The Greek word translated as load is *phortion*. It means the portion that must be carried or borne by an individual. The idea is of a duty or task that *belongs* to a specific person. In modern English we would call this type of weight *personal responsibility*.

Let me share a fanciful story to illustrate the difference between these two concepts. Imagine that you're driving down a rough and muddy road in a horse-drawn wagon. Before you know it, you hit a rut and land sideways in a ditch. But, lucky for you, I come galloping along on my white stallion.

"Not to worry," I exclaim. "Climb back into your wagon and I'll take care of everything." Confusing myself with Superman, I assume responsibility for lifting you, your horse and your wagon out of the ditch.

Sounds far fetched and unrealistic, doesn't it? But it's exactly what I'm trying to do when I take over your rightful portion of responsibility or *phortion*. In other words, I assume that you're totally incapable of helping yourself; so I take charge, demonstrating in the process an inflated picture of my own wisdom, strength and abilities and a very low opinion of yours.

Now imagine the same wagon in a ditch, only the story has a different ending. This time, aware of my own limitations and your responsibilities, I offer to come alongside and work with you to push the wagon out of the ditch. We both put our shoulders to the wheel and work together to get the wagon free.

The biblical concept of helping calls me to share your burden or *baros*, but the responsibility or *phortion* for your own life and your load of problems still belongs to you. In this scenario, I recognize that you need help and I offer assistance. Although you're ultimately in charge of the outcome, I'm willing to work with you to help you solve your problem. It might be helpful to remember that even when I help you out, it's still your problem or concern rather than mine.

In real life, it's healthy and compassionate to come alongside others and help them to shoulder their emotional, spiritual and physical burdens. The point at which helping becomes unhealthy or codependent, however, is when I assume your obligations and take them as my own. A practical example is raising children. Of course, the responsibility of caring for a child belongs to his own mother and father. It's their load. However, caring friends, grandparents or relatives may choose to come alongside to help with diapers, laundry and the other daily *burdens* associated with child rearing. This kind of burden bearing expresses true compassion, but load bearing is inappropriate.

Diaper changing and baby-sitting are helpful; but if I decide to "help you" by taking away custody of your children, it wouldn't be compassion — it would be kidnapping!

Problem Ownership

To be healthy and helpful to others, then, we must learn the secret of effective problem ownership. Helpers who avoid taking monkeys and succeed in keeping the problem focused in the right place can powerfully minister life, hope and peace to others without being burned out in the process.

When it comes to problem ownership, there are only four basic options:

1. **I own the problem.** In this case, I am responsible for taking action to solve or deal with my problem.

    Example:

    I want to take a day off work, but I don't feel comfortable asking my employer for the time off.

142

Unhealthy Response:

My boss should know that I've been working too hard. She should give me the day off without my having to ask for it! It's her fault that I'm feeling so burned out lately.

I try to transfer responsibility for my problem to some one else and blame her for my actions and feelings.

Healthy Response:

I feel worn-out! Even though I'm a little bit afraid, I need to ask my boss for a day off. I believe I deserve it.

I recognize my needs and own my feelings and perceptions. Even though my employer may not respond the way I'd like her to, I'm responsible for dealing with my problem.

2. **You own the problem.** If it's your problem, you're responsible for taking action to solve or deal with it.

Example:

You have a writing project that's due tomorrow, but you don't have time to type it.

Unhealthy Response:

If you don't help me type this project, I'll be in big trouble! If you really care about me, you'll do it for me.

You try to shift responsibility and anxiety for your problem on to me and make rescuing you a test of my love for you to boot.

Healthy response:

I have a problem. My project is due tomorrow and I don't have time to type it. Would you be willing to help me with it?

You're responsible for your own project and the consequences of turning it in late. Asking for help is appropriate as long as you're willing to take no for an answer.

3. **We own the problem.** We have a shared responsibility for dealing with it and finding solutions together.

Example:

While serving on the church mission committee, we've been given the task of choosing groups that we'll support in the coming year. More worthy organizations are asking for help than we can possibly support financially.

Unhealthy Response:

I can't bear the thought of disappointing all those poor missionaries! Whatever we do, we're going to upset somebody. You're a hard-nosed, tough-minded businessman. . . you decide for us.

Instead of sharing the accountability for difficult decisions, it's tempting to abdicate your share of responsibility. Avoiding and shifting blame for painful decisions leads to scapegoating.

Healthy Response:

It sure is hard to decide which groups to support, knowing that we're going to have to disappoint so many good people. I'm having a hard time deciding without my feelings taking over. I could use your help in looking at the different groups more objectively before we decide which ones to support.

We have joint responsibility for finding a resolution to shared problems; but each person still retains individual responsibility for his own thoughts, feelings and input. We must negotiate and work together.

4. **There is no problem.** No solution is necessary. There are times when we assume there are problems when none exist. Sometimes people share a problem they have already resolved. If we jump to conclusions and try to solve it for them, we cause ourselves needless anxiety.

Monkeying Around

I recently met a woman who was deeply concerned for her daughter. The daughter had real difficulty getting up in the morning and getting to school. The mother had made a daily ritual out of pleading, begging and fighting with her daughter to get her out of bed. This may not sound too unusual to other parents reading this book; but in this case, the daughter was 25 years old, attending graduate school and engaged to be married! The mother was extremely anxious about what would happen after her daughter moved out and got married. She wasn't sure she could trust her new son-in-law to "take care" of getting her daughter up and off to school.

In terms of problem ownership, whose responsibility was it to get the daughter up in the morning? Certainly oversleeping was the daughter's problem, but her mother had taken on her child's monkey. You can see how, by assuming all of the responsibility and anxiety for getting her daughter off to school, Mom was actually encouraging dependence and immaturity; and, if the adult child missed school, guess who she would blame.

Codependency And Monkeys

In recent years there have been hundreds of studies, articles and books on the topic of codependency. Several years before the term was popularized in books such as Claudia Black's *It Will Never Happen to Me*[2] or Robin Norwood's *Women Who Love Too Much*,[3] we were teaching the same idea but called it "problem ownership" and "monkey shifting."

The term codependency was originally coined by therapists working with the families of alcoholics. They recognized that

145

the alcoholic's family played a key role in supporting and enabling the addictive cycle. They saw that while alcoholics and addicts are chemically dependent, their family members also frequently became hooked or *codependent* on certain emotional and behavioral patterns. Chief among these patterns is assuming practical and emotional responsibility for the behaviors and feelings of others. This is what I call carrying their monkeys. Obviously, it isn't only children from alcoholic families who struggle with it.

My friend Dr. Margaret J. Rinck (author of *Can Christians Love Too Much?*) writes that Christians seem to be especially susceptible to confusing compassion with the unhealthy patterns of codependency:

> *Scripture does speak of denial and self-sacrifice, make no mistake about it. However, we need to distinguish clearly between true biblical servanthood and narcissistic codependent love which causes us to lose our identity.*[4]

Codependency, or "loving too much," Dr. Rinck writes, has another distinguishing feature:

> *It involves compulsion rather than choice. A person who loves too much does so out of fear or because he "has to." When I love you, serve you, help you, simply because I am afraid that you will be mad at me, leave me, abuse me, or dislike me, then my love is not freely chosen.*[5]

When we feel compelled to take on other people's monkeys, we're on our way to becoming compulsive caretakers or what I call *need-aholics*. That's when we desperately *need to be needed* by others so much that we sacrifice our true identities in an unavailing effort to gain approval from others, from ourselves and/or even from God. I say *unavailing* because our need for acceptance is insatiable. That's why all helping must be firmly built on an understanding of God's complete and unconditional acceptance of us and of those with whom we're working.

The Origin Of Monkeys

To illustrate, let me open the Sweeten family scrapbook and give you a first-hand look at how I became a monkey carrier early on.

Like most children, I assumed various roles according to the different situations I found myself in. Back home in southern Illinois, I earned a reputation as a rebellious little rascal. One of my nicknames was Jesse James. Does that give you an idea of what I was like as a kid?

Within the church and school setting, however, and whenever I spent time with my grandparents who lived next door, I shifted myself amazingly into the role of a rescuer or hero.

Around my grandparents' house I got my strokes from being Grandmother's conscientious little helper. I deeply wanted her approval and would do almost anything to please her. For instance, during the last six or seven years of his life, my grandfather was a semi-invalid. From the time I was in the first grade, I'd rush home after school every day and go next door to take care of him so my grandmother could attend to her grocery store chores and "church work." Because I spent every afternoon and evening at my grandfather's house, I didn't go out to play with the other kids. Even though I wanted to play, my need for affirmation drove me to being the family's caretaker.

When I went to church with my grandmother, my growing "monkey addiction" was only reinforced. To me, being a Christian came to mean taking care of everybody's needs — *except my own.* Of course, I was meeting my *need to be needed* by making myself indispensable, so I got a lot of strokes from the church people and my parents. "What a beautiful thing to do!" they would say. Unfortunately, their well-intentioned praise for my overfunctioning encouraged my codependency and my monkey-carrying.

Confused Compassion

As a youngster, I was attracted to a life style of excessive working and overfunctioning, and even today it's a temptation.

My security, identity and my Christianity were all wrapped up in doing for others instead of being in relationship with God. Like many folks, I was operating out of some pretty warped assumptions about compassion and Christianity.

For instance, although I never articulated them, I thought that the rules for being a good Christian required that I should always:

- Have the right answers.
- Be in control of the situation.
- Be able to make others' pain go away.
- Always be available.
- Always be nice.

Through a combination of humbling experiences, overwhelming stress and reading the Bible for myself, I'm learning to operate on a different set of assumptions.

Now as a Christian, I realize:

- I can't be all knowing. Only God is.
- I'm not always in control of everything. God is in charge.
- I can't make the pain go away. God can take pain away or use it for good.
- I'm often unavailable. But God is always there when we turn to Him.
- Being nice isn't always being truthful.

To overcome my monkey addiction, I'm learning to recognize the temptation in myself to "play God" by trying to solve everyone else's problems. I'm learning to resist the urgent inner impulse and family conditioning to fix other people. This way I can pay attention to areas I need to grow in so I can be more helpful to others in need. When I act on my inner compulsions, the behavior is aimed at lowering my anxiety rather than meeting the needs of others.

This is what Jesus was talking about in Matthew 7:3 when He taught His disciples how to be Helpers:

Why do you look at the speck of sawdust in your brother's eye and pay no attention to the plank in your own eye? How can you say to your brother, "Let me take the speck out of your eye," when all the time there is a plank in your own eye? You hypocrite, first take the plank out of your own eye, and then you will see clearly to remove the speck from your brother's eye.

The first step to effective helping is self-improvement. The word hypocrite means "one who wears a mask." So, take off the mask that covers up your own needs and problems and get real. Then, and only then, can you see clearly enough to do eye surgery.

Part of the reason we, as loving Christians, can get so confused is because we equate being responsible *for* others with being responsible *to* others. A number of years ago, Gail Ellis, a Stephen's Minister at Lakewood Presbyterian Church in Lakewood, Ohio, shared this helpful concept with us:

When I feel responsible FOR others:

I. . .
- Fix.
- Protect.
- Rescue.
- Control.
- Carry their feelings.
- Don't listen.

I feel. . .
- Tired.
- Anxious.
- Fearful.
- Liable.

I am concerned with. . .
- The solution.
- The answer.
- Circumstances.
- Being right.
- Details.
- Performance.

I am a manipulator.

I expect the person to live up to my expectations.

When I feel responsible TO others:

I...
- Show empathy.
- Encourage.
- Share.
- Confront.
- Am sensitive.
- Listen.

I feel. . .
- Relaxed.
- Free.
- Aware.
- High self-worth.

I am concerned with. . .
- Relating person-to-person as an equal to others.
- Listening to their feelings and thoughts.
- Respecting the person.

I am a helper/guide.

I can trust, let go.[6]

How To Handle Monkeys

Sounds great, doesn't it? So how do we get down off our stallions and start handling monkeys in a healthy, Christ-centered manner? How can we discover the difference between helpful Christian compassion and unhealthy codependency? Here are some suggestions:

- **Listen** *for heaven's sake*. As a Helper, approach those who are seeking with a willingness to listen with *warmth*, *empathy* and *respect*.

- **Identify the monkey**. What is the problem or situation?

- **Clarify**. Gently establish whose monkey it is. Is it yours? Mine? Ours? Or nobody's?

    If it's your monkey, then I must gently let you know you have my support. I'll come alongside you as a paraclete, but only you can ultimately work out your own issues.

    If it's my monkey, I will have to face the responsibility for taking care of it, perhaps with your support.

    If it's a joint problem, as is the case in many situations, then we will work together to find a mutually acceptable solution.

    If it's nobody's monkey (sometimes people perceive problems when they don't really exist), then thank God!

- **Delay decisions**. When you're not sure if you're taking someone else's monkey, slow down the process. You might say something like, "Can I think about this and get back to you?" This gives you the time to overcome peer pressure and to avoid making an unhealthy response. You may need to pray about whether you're yielding to compassion or to your own codependency.

- **Affirm and empower**. Affirm the Seeker's ability to handle the situation, and pray for God's power to bring success.

And Stay Off The Stallions!

While Christian compassion is both healthy and helpful, it's not always simple. Several years ago, I was in North Carolina teaching *Breaking Free From The Past* [7] at a conference. Since it was a short seminar and there wasn't a lot of time for modeling, I set some clear-cut boundaries on what we could and could not do in our time together as a small group. My temptation, of course, was to try to meet everyone's needs in the three-hour time period.

At the close of the seminar, a woman who had not received prayer during the time I had set aside approached me. "I've been thinking about a lot of things we've discussed here today, and I want you to pray for me. Since I live in Cincinnati, can you meet me when we get home? Then we won't be inhibited by this time limit."

Without hesitating, I enthusiastically responded, "Well, of course!" Thankfully, one of the other group members brought me back to earth by saying: "Gary, why don't you meet her right outside the O.K. Corral? Isn't that where you keep your white horse?"

Like a laser beam the truth of her comment struck home, and the humor encouraged us all to laugh at my unconscious compulsion to take the lady's monkey while riding a white horse!

If you're wondering whether you might have a monkey problem too, you could benefit from this scale developed by Jan Gossner, a theologian from Oslo, Norway. It may help you assess your level of responsibility or codependency. Think about where you would fit on the scale by asking yourself the questions below. Place the number that best describes your answer in the space provided.

Responsibility Checklist

Total Lack of Responsibility 1	Under Responsible 2	Peaceful Relaxed Responsible 3	Over Responsible 4	Hyper Responsible 5

As a child, I was _____ *3* .

Mother would say I was _____ *3* .

Dad would say I was _____ *5* .

My spouse would say I was _____ *5* .

I say I am at _____ *4* today.

I want to be _____ *3* as soon as possible.

Our goal is to move toward peaceful, relaxed and responsible relationships.

When do you think you have been able to move toward more health? What did you do? Could you do it again?

How could you move toward peace?

It's easy to get out of balance when internal and external expectations begin to take control. As we have mentioned in the first chapter, the secret of staying healthy and balanced depends on keeping God at the center of your life. The next chapter will provide some basic guidance for learning to listen to God.

No Monkeys

Listening to God's Voice

Steve woke up one Monday morning feeling very discouraged. His ministry as pastor of a large and growing congregation seemed to be going extremely well. . . more people were coming to Christ every week. . . his writings were receiving international recognition. . . he was getting speaking invitations from churches all over the world. Lately, however, he found himself dreaming about quitting the ministry and becoming a used car dealer.

As he often does when he needs to think, Steve got in his car and went out for a long drive. Pouring out his heart to God, Steve told Him how inadequate he felt faced with the overwhelming needs people were bringing to him as a pastor. Steve finally gave voice to his inner doubts saying, "God I'm not sure that I can do what you want me to do. Maybe I don't really have a pastor's heart."

By this time Steve was pulling into the drive-through lane of a Taco Bell restaurant to get something to eat. In the time between shouting his order into the microphone and picking it up from the service window, God spoke to Steve.

God said, "Open your door; I have a present for you." Feeling a little embarrassed, Steve stopped his car and opened his door. Ground into the pavement below him was a scarred and tarnished penny. As he dug the worn and blemished coin from the soft asphalt, God spoke again: "Steve, the people who are coming to you are like this penny. In the eyes of the world around them they don't have much value. In their own eyes they are shabby and worthless, but to Me they are precious beyond measure!"

Tears running down his face, Steve drove toward home with a penny, a bag of tacos and a whole new understanding of God's heart for people. "It's a funny thing," Steve told me later in an awestruck tone. "Several times since that Monday morning, as I've talked to hurting people, when I looked down at my feet I have discovered another penny! I have a whole stack of those pennies on my desk to remind me of God's heart for people and His special calling on my life."

Does God Really Speak to People?

Steve's story powerfully communicates God's love, but it also raises some important questions for many of our readers. Let's begin with the most basic question: does God speak to people?

If we accept the Old and New Testaments as more than a compilation of interesting fables or ancient fairy tales, we must also embrace the Scriptural portrayal of a God who gets personally involved with His creation. From Genesis to Revelation, the Bible is the story of everyday people who talked to, argued with, obeyed, disobeyed and ignored God.

Take a look at the list of biblical characters below. They came from widely diverse backgrounds. They were farmers, fisherman, scholars, soldiers, priests, politicians, prophets, tax gatherers, murderers and kings. Separated in time by hundreds of years, they had one significant experience in common. They all heard from God.

• Adam	• Eve	• Cain	• Noah
• Abraham	• Sarah	• Hagar	• Isaac
• Jacob	• Joseph	• Moses	• Pharaoh
• Joshua	• Gideon	• Samuel	• David
• Nathan	• Solomon	• Elijah	• Elisha
• Job	• Isaiah	• Jeremiah	• Ezekiel
• Daniel	• Hosea	• Joel	• Amos
• Obadiah	• Jonah	• Micah	• Nahum
• Habakkuk	• Zephaniah	• Haggai	• Malachi
• Zechariah	• Mary	• Joseph	• Peter

- The Wise Men
- John the Baptist

- John
- Phillip

- Martha
- Paul

- Stephen
- Ananias

How Does God Speak?

The theme of our book is listening, but thus far we have spent most of our time in learning how to listen to others and ourselves more effectively. If we desire healthy balance in our relationships, we must also learn to listen to God's voice. But how does God speak?

You don't need to be a Bible scholar to understand that God has revealed Himself to all sorts of human beings over the course of time. The author of the Book of Hebrews tells us that God has spoken *"at many times and in various ways"* (Hebrews 1:1) with the purpose of disclosing Himself and His will to humankind. The Bible chronicles some rather creative methods God has used to get His messages through to people, including a wrestling angel (Genesis 32:24), a burning bush (Exodus 3:2), a raging whirlwind (Job 38:1) and even a talking donkey (Numbers 22:28).

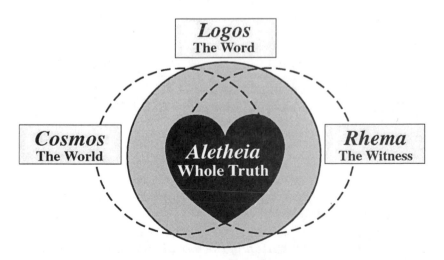

Three Channels God Uses to Communicate Truth

While God has used extraordinary modes of communication in specific instances, there seem to be three basic channels of communication described in the Bible. Using New Testament Greek terminology, we can say that God speaks to us through His **world** (*Cosmos*), His **word** (*Logos*) and His **witness** (*Rhema*). God uses all three of these channels to communicate the fullness of His truth (*Aletheia*) to people like you and me. Let's start with *Cosmos*, God's most universal method for communicating Himself to humanity. How does God use the Creation to communicate with us?

Cosmos: The World

An eight-year-old boy interrupted his father's television watching one beautiful Sunday afternoon with a momentous question: "Dad, do you believe in God?"

Startled by the unexpected nature of his son's question, the father switched off the TV. His brows knit together in a troubled expression and with painful honesty the father replied, "I really don't know, Son." The boy looked at him with an expression of complete assurance and said: "There has to be a God, Dad ! Somebody had to make the grass and the trees and the stars and stuff. There's no way all of it happened by itself."

Although the father wasn't aware of it, his son was simply pointing out the same truth expressed in the Psalms and the book of Romans:

> The heavens declare the glory of God; the skies proclaim the work of his hands. Day after day they pour forth speech; night after night they display knowledge. (Psalm 19:1, 2)

> For since the creation of the world God's invisible qualities—his eternal power and divine nature—have been clearly seen, being understood from what has been made, so that men are without excuse. (Romans 1:20)

156

In an exciting demonstration of how God can speak through the created world or ***Cosmos***, the conversation between the little boy and his father led them in a search to identify the architect of the heavens. The father came up with an idea: "Let's write God a letter and ask Him to send us someone who can answer our question." After writing the letter together, they tied it to a helium filled balloon and let it loose and watched it ascend into the sky above them.

Two weeks later, they drove into a local gas station. A gentleman nearby started washing their windshield. Seeing that he did not have on a uniform from the station, the father asked, "If you don't work here, why are you doing this?" The man smiled and said, "I'm doing this to show you in a practical way that God loves you." The father and son looked at each other in stunned silence, then turned to the man and said, "We want to know more about God. Can you help us?" "Why, yes," he answered. "I'm the pastor from the church down the street. Come and see me any time." Recently both father and son were baptized on the same day.

Science and *Cosmos*

The intricacies and the arrangement of what God has made "pour forth speech" night and day creating a hunger in us to understand more of our Creator. The mysteries of the Cosmos seem to be designed to evoke curiosity about God. Modern science as we know it began with inquisitive Christians seeking to better understand God through studying His creation. Gregor Mendel, an Austrian monk, believed that even the smallest and seemingly least significant components of God's design contain divine revelation. Mendel is credited with establishing the science of genetics by studying the intricacies of plants and their reproduction. Other notable scientists such as Galileo Galilei, Blaise Pascal and Sir Isaac Newton also believed that studying the laws of the physical universe can lead to a deeper understanding of the intentions of its Creator.

157

Even the most renowned scientist of the 20th century believed that scientific study provides insight into a Divine Creator. Albert Einstein stood in reverence before a universe he believed to express divine creativity saying: "One cannot help but be in awe when he contemplates the mysteries of eternity, of life, of the marvelous structure of reality. He who can no longer pause to wonder and stand rapt in awe, is as good as dead; his eyes are closed." He counseled aspiring scientists never to lose the "holy curiosity" that leads to exploring and understanding how God expresses Himself through the universe around us.

Eminent surgeon, medical researcher and Christian author Dr. Paul Brand has written two wonderful books with Phillip Yancey. *Fearfully and Wonderfully Made*[1] and *In His Image*[2] illustrate the power of listening to the *cosmos*. Dr. Brand's words are inspiring as he explains how God used 20 years of Brand's medical knowledge and clinical practice in India to reveal more about Himself.

One of the illustrations in *In His Image* compares God's capacity to hear the prayers of so many people to the communication between the brain and our body cells:

> *Of all the marvelous aspects of the human body, I know of no greater wonder than that every one of the hundred trillion cells in my body has access to the brain. Many cells, such as those used in sight, have direct neuronal connections; others have channels immediately available to them to report in on their needs or current states. And in the Body of Christ, I know of no greater wonder than that each one of us has direct contact with Christ Himself, the Head. Amazingly, He listens to our input, considers our requests, and quite literally uses that information to influence His direction of activities in the world.*[3]

Clearly there are theological lessons latent in the most modest of God's creations. This is no surprise to those who are familiar with Scriptural teaching. Jesus frequently took His explanations of God's Kingdom from the everyday sights, sounds and experiences of His listeners. He often pointed to natural illustrations such as.

- *Look at the birds of the air.* (Matthew 6:26)
- *See how the lilies of the field grow.* (Matthew 6:28)
- *Every good tree bears good fruit.* (Matthew 7:17)
- *A farmer went out to sow his seed.* (Matthew 13:3)
- *You know how to interpret the appearance of the sky.* (Matthew 16:3)
- *If you have faith as small as a mustard seed.* (Matthew 17:20)
- *Now learn this lesson from the fig tree.* (Mark 13:28)
- *Unless a kernel of wheat falls to the ground and dies.* (John 12:24)

Listening to Your Life

Jesus used these down-to-earth illustrations to reinforce ideas that God has been quietly communicating to us all along through His creation. Many people I talk to expect God to speak with a thunderous voice talking from the mountain tops accompanied by wind and flame like a scene from Cecil B. DeMille's *The Ten Commandments*. As Elijah discovered (1 Kings 19:11-12) God's voice isn't always found in dramatic devices such as mighty winds, shattering earthquakes or the consuming fires. Instead, God speaks with unexpected softness to most of us. He uses what Scripture calls a "still small voice" or a "whisper."

In her book *Listening For a God Who Whispers*,[4] Peggy Benson describes this aspect of listening to God through paying close attention to His *Cosmos*. She calls it "listening to your life." She encourages us to become aware of the "sound and the rhythm" of our lives and the lives around us so we can hear the voice of God gently speaking to us. But first, she tells us, we must learn to make friends with silence:

> *I have finally come to understand that it is only in the silence that I can hear the story of my life and the voice of God talking to me through the telling of it.*

If I will take the time to listen to my life, I can see where I have been and where I am going.

If I have the courage to listen to it, really listen to it, I can hear God speak to me about where I am now, not just about where I was back when my story was fresh and new and beginning.

If I will just be quiet and listen, I can hear him whisper to me about the story of my life that is being written this moment. About the needs and dreams and cares and joys and pains that were here an hour ago, and are going to be among the things I am going to need and want to remember and treasure in years to come.

God often speaks to us in the simple events of our daily lives. Pam's earliest experience in her desire to hear the Lord, illustrates this.

As someone who grew up in the church, I had often heard or read testimonies that started, "God told me....," and I could not say I'd ever heard God speak to me. So on a leadership retreat during an open prayer time, I asked God to teach me something personal. I was struggling in the glaring awareness of my sins, and felt unworthy of hearing God.

As I walked the retreat grounds, I saw a beautiful purple flower. It captured my attention so acutely, I decided to pick it. As I drew closer and reached for it, my hand recoiled at the huge thistle thorns surrounding the flower. I covered my hands with the tail of my shirt to avoid being pricked because I just had to have that flower. Just after picking it, the thought came through my mind: "Just as you see the beauty in this flower despite the thorns, I love you even in the midst of your sin." I was flabbergasted, and would have hesitated to say God had spoken. But the lesson of that moment remains with me today, over fifteen years later!

Scripture tells us that God is constantly speaking to us, but like Pam we may doubt our ability to accurately hear His voice. How can we tell if thoughts and impressions such as Pam describes are actually from God?

Logos: The Word

To answer this question, we must first understand the second and most important channel of interaction God uses to communicate with us. It is His *Logos* or living word. The meaning of *Logos* is the expression of an idea or personality behind the words. When we talk about Scripture being *alive,* we mean that God uses it to communicate in the here and now. The *Logos* is the power of the Holy Spirit inhabiting the inspired or *God-breathed* words of Scripture.

Scripture is God's special and permanent revelation of Himself to us. I am constantly astonished by how well a book written by authors who passed away thousands of years ago can speak so powerfully and directly to what is happening in my life at the moment. When I have an impression such as the one Pam shared above (or any idea about God for that matter), I turn to the pages of Scripture to confirm and test it. Is the message consistent with the character of Jesus? Does it seem consistent with the voice of God as revealed throughout the Bible? Will what I have just heard or thought lead me to grow in my relationship with God, myself and others?

Whatever the situation, the Bible is a dependable guide providing wisdom and direction when I need it. At work, at home, in my relationships and in my ministry I find what is written in the Bible is always relevant to my needs. As the Apostle Paul wrote to his young friend Timothy, "All Scripture is God-breathed and is useful for teaching, rebuking, correcting and training in righteousness" (2 Timothy 3:16). I have come to the conclusion that *every* word in both the Old and New Testaments is there for a reason.

Within the Scriptures themselves we find constant references to other passages and books of the Bible. The New Testament is built on the foundation of Old Testament Scripture and begins by showing how Jesus fulfills prophesies from Genesis to Malachi. Jesus himself validated the Old Testament Scriptures by quoting them frequently. He launched His earthly ministry by quoting Isaiah 61:1 and even quoted from Psalm 22:1 as he suffered the agony of the cross.

Passages that confused or seemed contradictory to me years or months ago have come alive as I have needed to apply them to my life. In the last chapter we discussed one of these "confusing" passages when it talked about carrying each other's burdens but not carrying each other's loads. The truth contained in that apparent contradiction has yielded a powerful insight and led to greater peace for many. While it is tempting to disregard or gloss over passages that we don't understand or don't agree with, we must understand that the tapestry of Scripture is a complete and integrated whole. If I tamper with or remove a single thread, I risk unraveling or distorting the picture God intended.

It's very dangerous to take Scripture out of context: to focus on a single passage while ignoring the fabric it is a part of. I grew up hearing many religious people attempt to justify racial segregation using selected passages from the Bible. I remember one man telling me that he believed that all Black people were *intended* to be slaves because there were slaves in both the Old and New Testaments. He was deeply offended when I pointed out that most of the slaves referred to in the Scriptures weren't black at all. They were mostly Hebrews, Greeks, Romans, and European Caucasians.

I have heard it said that "A *text*, without the *context* is a *pretext* for doing whatever you were going to do anyhow." Incalculable damage has been done by individuals attempting to use isolated verses from the Bible to support their personal prejudices and predetermined positions. I often hear radio preachers expounding on how good wives are to be perpetually subordinate to their husbands' desires even when those desires are hurtful and unreasonable. To justify a male dominant position, these men generally quote Ephesians 5:22 saying, "Wives, submit to your husbands as to the Lord."

Somehow these gentlemen conveniently omit the verse that immediately precedes this: Ephesians 5:21. It reads, "Submit to one another out of reverence for Christ." As a counselor, I have seen bushels of bitter fruit produced in marriages as a result of unbalanced teaching that leaves out the importance of *mutual* submission.

When we employ Scripture to excuse selfishness or justify a lack of personal compassion, we place ourselves in the same position as the Pharisees and Sadducees of the New Testament. I believe that Jesus would respond to us in the same way by saying, "You are in error because you do not know the Scriptures or the power of God" (Matthew 22:19).

The Law of Increasing Returns

To hear from God through the Scriptures, we can begin by reading them regularly, pondering what we read, and then personally applying what we hear. My experience has been that as we begin to use what we learn from the Bible it will come alive for us in powerful and challenging ways. Unlike the rest of life, where Murphy's Law reigns, when it comes to reading the Bible there is a law of *increasing returns*. The more we dig into the Scripture and use what we find, the more God uses it to speak to us.

Rhema: The Witness

The third means of hearing from God is expressed in the New Testament word **Rhema**. You may be familiar with the passage in Ephesians 6:17-19 that speaks of taking up "the sword of the Spirit, which is the word of God." You may not realize however, that the term translated as "the word of God" is *Rhema*. When Paul asks in the same passage that words may be given to him so that he can "fearlessly make known the mystery of the gospel," he is asking for *Rhema*. This is God's direct *witness* within us.

Rhema is supernatural revelation or words that God puts into your heart, your mind or your mouth for the purpose of making

163

known the mystery of the gospel. Unlike *Logos* words that are universal and permanent, *Rhema* words are intended for specific situations and people. *Rhema* words are both powerful and distinctive. Like a sword, they cut through our human confusion to provide clarity of thought and action. Most often in my experience, *Rhema* shows itself in the form of Scripture coming to my mind just when I need it.

Norway by Way of Kenya

It can also be an unexplainable personal insight into what God wants us to do in a particular situation. Once while I was serving on a committee with a group of leaders dedicated to bringing renewal to my denomination, my friend Brick Bradford had what I believe was a *Rhema* for me. While we were praying that God would renew His Church around the world, Brick said. "I have been invited to a conference in Kenya, Africa, on leading leaders; but I think Gary is supposed to go in my place."

I was surprised. I didn't know anything about this leaders' conference or about Africa. I wasn't even sure I could take the time off. I had lots of good reasons why I couldn't possibly go, but before Brick was finished speaking, somehow I also had a strange assurance that going to Africa was just the "right thing to do."

Six months later I arrived at the conference center near Nairobi with only a vague idea of what I was doing there. I recognize now that God had a divine appointment scheduled for me. In the dormitory where I was staying, I bunked next to a quiet, unassuming fellow from Oslo, Norway. This man, Jens-Petter Jorgensen, was an evangelist, a Bible school teacher and an important leader in the Norwegian renewal movement. One day as we rode the bus back from the conference to our dormitory, Jens-Petter stunned me by saying, "Gary, I think you are God's man for Norway."

Once I got over the shock, I asked him to explain. In a long conversation, Jens-Petter told me that he believed I had a special ministry and message for the Norwegian churches. Although I was somewhat astonished at the time, Jens-Petter's words turned out to be prophetic.

My "accidental" meeting with Jens-Petter in Nairobi has yielded extraordinary results in my life and in the lives of thousands of Scandinavians. After almost a decade of traveling to Scandinavia, speaking, leading ministry teams and helping to establish ongoing ministry there, I am very grateful for Brick Bradford's willingness to hear and to share a *Rhema* word that sent me to Norway by way of Africa. Looking back, I can see quite clearly how God has guided me over the years. Frankly, I am far less certain of which way to go in the future. This lack of certainty drives me to seek a balanced approach to hearing God.

The Search for Balance

God communicates in a variety of ways. Just as our nonverbals, our voice tone and our actual words are part of our everyday communication, God's *Cosmos*, *Rhema* and *Logos* are a normal part of His communication with us. But whether He speaks to us through the agency of His created order, Scripture or His Holy Spirit, God's personality and unfailing love always remain consistent.

When I was a young man, just out of graduate school, I was warned by Christian friends about paying too much attention to what scholars and scientists had to say. Book learning, in the anti-intellectual climate of many conservative churches, was considered antithetical to true Christian faith. Reading any book other than the Bible was bound to lead you astray. In my experience it turned out that this was far from true. The more I studied God's revelation in nature, the more I grew to trust in the God of Scripture. There are many times my heart jumped for joy when I read about the practices, principles and tools discovered by counselors which were obviously consistent with biblical ideas.

When it comes to hearing God, we can easily get out of balance by focusing too much of our attention on either the *Cosmos* or the *Rhema* and not paying enough attention to the *Logos*. Although each is important, the *Logos* is central to healthy growth because it gives us a tool for assessing and interpreting both the *Rhema* and the *Cosmos*.

If we rely too much on the *Cosmos* (the outer world of nature and science) to shape our understanding of God and His Will, we easily get off track. We can become mere worshipers of nature or followers of men. On the other hand, if we rely too much on *Rhema* (the inner world of subjective experience) to comprehend God, we become overly introspective, mystical and "so heavenly-minded we are no earthly good."

A healthy understanding of the *Logos* (Scripture) allows the richness of *Cosmos* and the power of *Rhema* to be expressed, while keeping our minds and hearts squarely rooted in the special revelation of His Word.

So again we return to *teleios, the* primary goal of Christian caring and counseling. As we listen and obey, we will begin to break free from those things that hinder us from a full experience of life, health and relationships.

Jesus tells us, ". . . if you continue in my word, then you are my disciples indeed; and you shall know the truth [*Aletheia*], and the truth shall make you free" (John 8:31, 32 KJV). *Aletheia* translates literally as the "unveiled reality." So what is this unveiled reality that God uses to release us from the ideas and things that hold us captive? What does Jesus mean when He says that by experiencing this reality we shall know liberty. Is freedom found in:

- The World of God's *Cosmos*?
- The Word of God's *Logos*?
- The Witness of God's *Rhema*?

The answer is "Yes!" God reveals His truth to us in all three ways. Our freedom comes as a result of allowing God's full truth to speak in our lives. Our part is simply to listen. Remember, we are young children who have been adopted by a heavenly Father who speaks a language very foreign from the one that we have learned. Don't be surprised if it takes a long time to learn that heavenly tongue. Give yourself grace for experiencing these three Be-attitudes. I have learned that observing these helps me tremendously as I seek to hear God's voice more clearly in my life:

Be Still

"Be still before the LORD and wait patiently for him" (Psalm 37:7). One of my great weaknesses as a very busy believer is an overall inability to be still. I rush around and often don't know how to slow down long enough to hear God or anyone else. In my experience, haste and anxiety are the enemies of listening to God and other people. The Lord wants us to learn to relax. He ordained the Sabbath day as a day of rest and relaxation for our bodies and for listening for the voice of the Holy Spirit.

I've heard it said that the devil is the only one who never takes a day off. Even God rested on the seventh day.

Be Quiet

"He makes me lie down in green pastures, He leads me beside quiet waters, He restores my soul" (Psalm 23:2, 3). I am an extrovert. I find talking much easier than listening. If there is silence, I am tempted to fill it with talking, singing or praying. Over the last few years, I have been learning the importance of practicing silence. As the Psalmist relates, it is in the quiet times and places I find refreshment, renewal and restoration.

Most of us learn our native language by listening to our parents when we are very young. How can we expect to learn our Heavenly Father's language if we never quiet down long enough to learn how He speaks? Some people call this process "making space for God." By developing habits of the heart which allow us to meditate on what God is telling us, we will be more likely to hear when He speaks.

Be Responsive

Do not merely listen to the word, and so deceive yourselves. Do what it says. Anyone who listens to the word but does not do what it says is like a man who looks at his face in a mirror and, after looking at himself, goes away and immediately forgets what he looks like. (James 1:22)

In our modern age we would say "use it or lose it."

The surest means to grow in your ability to hear God's voice is to respond to what you *do* understand. As we listen and obey we will begin to recognize God's voice. As we apply what we learn, we grow in health, wholeness and Christian maturity. We can't make ourselves pure or healthy by ourselves, but with God's guidance and support, we can leave what is impure, harmful and unhealthy, and begin to walk in the truth that sets us free.

Like every other aspect of *Listening for heaven's sake,* consistently listening to God is a challenge. You may have to overcome lifelong habits that hinder you in your ability to slow down, quiet down, and get down to the business of healthy growth and change. Our next chapter will focus on successfully meeting some of those challenges as we seek to apply what we have learned.

The Challenge
of Growth

When Dave and Pam Ping went to the video store, it was Pam's turn to pick. So when she chose a romantic movie about figure skating, called *The Cutting Edge*,[1] Dave wasn't surprised at all. Although romance movies aren't Dave's first choice, he was pleasantly surprised with this one.

The story revolves around an ice hockey star, Doug Dorsey, who, because of a head injury, can no longer take the intense physical contact of the sport. An international figure skating coach recognizes his hidden potential to succeed in Olympic figure skating and teams him with a talented, but temperamental, young female ice star.

The early part of the movie focuses on Doug's struggle to move away from the power and speed necessary for hockey and to learn the control and finesse that dominates the sport of figure skating. Although he has the potential and the basic skills, he still feels extremely self-conscious learning and practicing the new techniques that are required of him. Hockey skates and figure skates are quite different, and it takes months of hard work and practice to break old habits. In many ways it's like learning to skate all over again with all the falls, bumps and spills that entails.

In some ways, Doug is facing the same basic paradox of growth and change that you and I must deal with as we apply the ideas contained in this book to our lives. We are moved and inspired by those who model listening and caring skills with seemingly effortless poise and expertise. They make it look so easy. When we try it ourselves, however, it's a different story altogether. Unfortunately, like anyone learning a new skill, we have to start at the beginning by learning and practicing the basics.

When I coached basketball, I always had a hard time convincing the guys how important practice drills are. In their excitement and enthusiasm, they didn't want to waste time on fundamental drills. . .they wanted to play basketball! They watched the college and professional basketball stars on TV and they were sure they could emulate all the dazzling moves they observed. They didn't understand that it's the basics, not the flashy moves, that win games.

In building healthy relationships, it's also the basics of warmth, empathy, respect, and appropriate problem ownership that win people over to caring and health. But these basics require the same kind of diligent practice that ice skating or soccer or basketball does, and there are the same resistances to change.

As I began to practice these skills in my own family and professional life, there was enormous resistance from within myself and from those around me. I had always seen myself as having more and better insights than almost anyone. My theme song in life was "Lord, It's Hard to be Humble, When You're Perfect in Every Way." To make matters worse, my temperament drives me to want to be competent above all else. These two things together caused enormous pressure to perform by telling others what I knew. Instead of listening to God and others, I overfunctioned by telling others what to do. I wasn't very warm, empathic or respectful.

Each time I read about helping skills and practiced them, I grew in understanding and ability; but it was a rough growth process. In fact, some of the people around me didn't like me or my attempts to listen at all. My son Tim was quite young at the time and challenged me when my skills were rough. Once, while riding in the car together, he told me in no uncertain terms to "quit that listening stuff." I had been spending so much time using the formula that I hadn't made the skills a genuine part of my life. Now, many years later, Tim told me that it was apparent to him that I wasn't just *using* active listening *on* people. I was, rather, listening because I was truly interested in them. After all these years of learning and working and growing as a Helper and a Seeker, it was exciting to hear Tim's encouraging feedback.

You were probably drawn to this book because you wanted to improve your listening and relational skills. You may have even had a particular relationship in mind. Whatever the reason, you brought many abilities that have served you well in the past. Like Doug from the movie *The Cutting Edge,* the challenge for you is to integrate old skills with new ones. To become the most effective Helper or Seeker you can be, you will probably have to break some familiar patterns and make room for new ones. Like me, you'll have to prove to the people closest to you that you are genuinely interested in them.

Starting from where you are now, how can you grow:

- To become a more effective Seeker?
- To become a more effective Helper?

The answer requires understanding of four fundamental stages for learning new behaviors:

- Unconscious Incompetence.
- Conscious Incompetence.
- Conscious Competence.
- Unconscious Competence.

Whenever we begin to learn anything new, we start at the stage of **Unconscious Incompetence**. We're unaware of critical behaviors that impede our effectiveness. Listening is a skill we've probably taken for granted our whole lives. We may not have been conscious of any problems or areas in need of improvement. One frequent comment we hear at our LIFE Seminars is " I always thought I was a pretty good listener until I took this course."

Now you've arrived at **Conscious Incompetence**. You probably feel self-conscious, uncomfortable and/or overwhelmed with the challenge of internalizing new ways of relating. Some become discouraged by this new insight into past patterns. But instead of dwelling on your inadequacies or deficiencies, you can gain hope and encouragement from the knowledge that "it is God who works in you to will and to act according to His good purpose" (Philippians 2:13). This is a very rough time, and many give up rather than continue the hard work necessary to move to the next stage.

After much practice and attention to developing foundational skills, we reach the stage of **Conscious Competence**. Just as training wheels are helpful in learning to ride a bicycle, the empathy formula, feeling words list (see the last page of this book) and tentative openings from the previous chapters can give you security as you mature in your ability to demonstrate caring, understanding and respect. This stage of learning is similar to reminding yourself how to shoot a basketball or kick a soccer ball. ("OK, Gary, take one more step, relax and put your foot at the bottom of the ball aimed right at the goal.") So I consciously think about what I need to do because it is still in the pre-habitual stage of learning.

Once we've fully integrated a new skill into our lives, it becomes natural and comfortable. When effective listening and caring become second nature, we've reached the skill level of **Unconscious Competence**. Even at this stage, however, we'll have room to improve; but at least it is now a part of our habit pattern. The more we use any skill, the more natural and developed it becomes.

Finding Encouragement

One of the most important factors in beginning new and healthier habits is encouragement or what scientists call *reinforcement*. People from all over the world attend our seminars, and many are concerned about how to live out the new behaviors at home where the people around them have not experienced the same training. I always recommend that graduates build a support system around themselves and pass on their new knowledge to a few others who can help them practice and grow.

I remember a behavior study from my graduate school days where groups of ten people were put in a room together. Nine of each group had been secretly coached to respond in a predetermined manner to questions a clinician would ask. Only one out of the ten would be responding on his own.

The clinician drew three lines of slightly different length labeled A, B and C. Each of the ten was asked consecutively to identify the shortest line. One by one the coached individuals responded that line A was the shortest, even though in reality, line B was clearly shorter. Eighty percent of the time the tenth individual would go along with the crowd, even though common sense indicated otherwise.

Then one of the coached participants in each group responded accurately. The results were dramatic. One hundred percent of the non-coached participants correctly identified the shortest line.

I mention this study to demonstrate the power of peer reinforcement. When we're alone in a decision we begin to question our own good judgment. When we're surrounded by unhealthy influences, it begins to feel as if we're swimming against the current. By drawing near to one person or several people who want to grow, we can improve our own health and chances for success.

As we mentioned in Chapter 1, Solomon reminds us in Ecclesiastes 4:9 that "a cord of three strands cannot easily be broken." Perhaps this is the reason that Jesus sent His disciples out two by two. Each one supported the other and both received encouragement and wisdom from God.

Johari Window

A graphic depiction of the benefits of sharing yourself with others both as a Helper and a Seeker is shown in the Johari Window. This model was originally developed by Joseph Luft and Harry Ingham and was labeled the Johari Window after their first names.[2] The model represents an individual by using four quadrants.

	Known to Self	Not Known to Self
Known to Others	1. Shared	2. Blind
Not Known to Others	3. Hidden	4. Unknown

The first quadrant symbolizes those areas of our self that are known both to ourselves and others. This is the shared area. As in the upside-down heart described in Chapter 2, this is the area we're comfortable sharing with the people we trust.

The second quadrant, or blind area, denotes the parts of self that are known to others but unknown to us. I call this the "bad breath" area. Some call it the "slip is showing" or the" zipper is down" area. Regardless of what we call it, it demonstrates our need for constructive feedback from other people. Even when this input is painful or embarrassing, it's extremely necessary for our personal growth. When we give others permission to hold us accountable and to be honest about both our strengths and weaknesses, health results.

Quadrant three includes the areas of our lives, thoughts and feelings that we know about but hide from others. I call this the "skeleton in the closet" area. Fear and shame tend to control this critical area and keep us in bondage. Often we avoid letting others close enough to peek in the closet. Only when the trust level is very high will I permit access to this hidden area.

The fourth quadrant represents areas unknown to others and to us about ourselves. Only God is completely aware of the hidden treasures and traumas contained here. The unknown mysteries located here are revealed as we develop a closer relationship with God, ourselves and others.

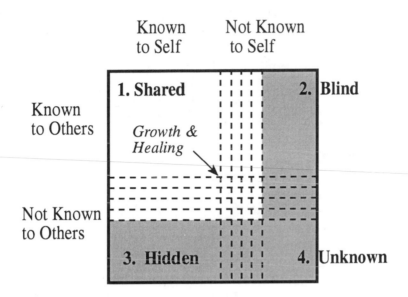

What makes the diagram above exciting is that it demonstrates a profound truth in a simple way: As we share ourselves with those that we can trust, we will see our blind area, hidden area and unknown area shrink significantly. The outcome is increased intimacy with others, increased understanding of ourselves and an increased experience of God's tenderness and caring in our lives.

The more we open our lives to God, to ourselves and to others in appropriate and healthy ways, the more healing, wholeness and joy can enter in. This window is a profound visualization of theology: a continuation of God's truth, fruit and gifts working together to minister to the whole person.

You have already begun a process of growth and movement toward health by reading the previous chapters. By now you may be aware of areas of your life that you would like to improve. You may be wondering, "What is the next step?"

Equipping yourself to be a better Helper and life-choosing Seeker requires practice. Didactic and reflective education does not. If you would like to continue growing, we would urge you not only to study the information contained here, but to put them into practice until effective listening and caring becomes a more natural inclination. Without adding the experiential, accountability and modeling aspect of the training model, health-giving behavior is almost impossible. Jesus taught, modeled and reflected. He also sent the team out to practice newly learned behaviors and then had the disciples return for supervision.

In our experience, the most effective place to begin is to incorporate the skills and attitudes you've learned in this book into your daily life. Research shows that it takes at least 30 days of constant repetition to learn a new habit. We encourage those who attend our LIFE Seminars to establish small groups to practice listening and caring skills with one another. There's a double benefit. Group participants not only improve their skills, many times they also develop deeper relationships with others in the group as they are willing to share their own lives, experiences and struggles. In other words, they fulfill the goals of this course by becoming better Helpers and better Seekers.

Arthur's Journey

In 1987, the White House Conference for a Drug-Free America was held in Washington, D.C. It attracted thousands of teenagers from across the country. One of the most popular speakers at the conference was a Pentagon official who told the story of a man named Arthur.

A big, burly man whose mere presence commanded respect, the speaker was both gentle and inspirational as he related the story to the enthralled youngsters.

Born into a poor African-American family, Arthur grew up in the streets of Washington, D.C. The son of divorced parents, he eventually joined the Army — just in time to fight in Vietnam. There he became addicted to alcohol and drugs, cocaine and heroin.

After his discharge from the military, he married; but his alcohol and chemical dependency habits contributed to an early divorce. Before he was out of his 20s, Arthur had hit rock bottom.

Arrested and placed in a treatment center, he began the long, slow process toward recovery. After years of rehabilitation, he beat his habits and was placed into a job. He was a janitor in the Pentagon.

In his new, healthier life, Arthur viewed himself and the world a lot differently from what he once had. He was determined to be the very best he could be — and that included being the absolutely best janitor the Pentagon had ever seen. To that end, he worked and cleaned and polished until he could see his face shine on the backs of the toilet seats he was in charge of cleaning.

Recognizing Arthur's dedication and exceptional work habits, his superiors promoted him, putting him in charge of cleaning a number of Pentagon offices.

Ah! Now he had a new goal. As unlikely as it might appear considering his past, Arthur decided that one day *his* name would hang on the door of one of those offices.

As he addressed an enthusiastic and awed crowd of American teenagers at that conference, the speaker revealed that he was, in fact, Arthur. He now held a position of responsibility and had his own office in our nation's Pentagon.

In his gentle, frank account of his journey into and out of the trenches and into a new life, Arthur told the youngsters in his audience that he's often asked how in the world he did it. In response, he enjoys sharing a picture puzzle analogy.

Arthur likens himself to the little boy whose father is working on a huge puzzle of the world. For days and days the father struggles to get the pieces to fit. But it's so huge and so complex that the challenge becomes frustrating. Finally, the little boy asks, "Dad, may I help?"

"Go ahead," the father says reluctantly. He leaves the room, thinking: "Fat chance he'll be able to put that thing together. I've been working on it for days."

A short time later the father comes back, and to his incredible astonishment, finds that his son has solved the puzzle!

"My gosh, Son! How in the world did you do that?" the astounded father asks.

"It was simple," the youngster explains. "You just turn all the pieces over. On the back, there's a picture of a man. When you put the man together, the whole world falls into place."

When we're open to looking at ourselves and recognizing the power in the person of Jesus Christ, we can move toward *teleios* and enter into healthy, helpful relationships with ourselves and others. This allows us to move from victims to victors. So much of modern life focuses on the ways we've been victimized and the awfulness of pain and dysfunction. As a therapist, I've had special training in assessing and naming these problems.

The Greatest Is Love

It's my strong conviction, however, that a lot of the modern psychology and recovery movements put so much emphasis on problems that they fail to find solutions. Yes, people have been victimized; but it's wrong and disrespectful to treat them merely as victims. Our goal is to equip all people with the basic tools they need to discover solutions to their problems for themselves.

Some of the most powerful words, and the most beautiful, are found in 1 Corinthians 13. That marvelous chapter in the Bible ends with a famous passage that keeps us moving toward the goal of *teleios* (wholeness): "And now these three remain: faith, hope and love. But the greatest is love."

Faith draws us to a personal relationship with God. Faith is not something that can be measured or compared to others. It is, rather, a way of thinking about the trust we have in a person — God. Faith comes from the heart, for the focus is on being persuaded that God is a father and friend. So faith draws us toward confidence, hope, peace and self-esteem. The cause of faith is God. The Spirit of God gives us faith, and the object of our faith is God Himself. He alone is the Alpha and the Omega, the beginning and the end of faith.

Hope is the expectation of something good with the surety of its happening. "And hope does not disappoint us, because God has poured out His love into our hearts by the Holy Spirit, whom He has given us" (Romans 5:5). A wonderful term and an exciting prospect for believers, hope gives us the strength to move beyond the past to the present and the future. Otherwise, we could not genuinely encourage people to move from victim to victor.

"And the greatest is love." How sad it is for the church of Jesus Christ to be known for exclusion and rejection rather than for acceptance and inclusion. Therapeutic communities have two characteristics. First, they have what scholars call *communitas*, which summarizes godly love. *Communitas* is an attitude that translates into behavior. It is, first, an attitude of acceptance. People are accepted and respected for *Whose* they are, not what they do. Entry into the a healthy community or group allows and encourages folks to be "real" and to openly state their needs, differences and even their failures.

The love of God shown in us is so powerful that although it accepts us as we are, it won't leave us there. The family of God loves and confronts people into maturity and away from Sin. Agape love is both care and confrontation. It is love that has both the oil and the sandpaper of the Lord.

Just as a biological family must exhibit both tender and tough love, so must we in the family of God. And just as the biological family lives on for generations, so does the family of God. New members are constantly joining each family, providing a constant stream of people to love and to train. These same people need both care and confrontation.

Healing *charisma* focuses on the notion that growth and healing come through the community *and not just the leaders*. As members live out the truth, the fruit and the gifts God has developed in them, every member of the community is encouraged to move on and acquire more of the healing and grace God has for them. As we receive healing ourselves, we are able to pass it on to others. We are not only accepted as wounded individuals, we are encouraged to grow through our woundedness to become "wounded healers".

So we have come full circle. Once again we return to the story of nine-year-old Anna Marie and her perilous Atlantic crossing. If you think back to page 1 of this book, perhaps you will remember the secret Anna Marie's mother communicated so powerfully to her during her sea voyage to America. It's a secret Anna Marie never forgot: *THE COMFORT AND ENCOURAGEMENT WE RECEIVE FROM GOD IS MEANT TO BE SHARED WITH OTHERS*. If we allow Him to, and we are willing to share what God gives us, He will touch others with His comfort and his healing through us:

> *God is able to make all grace abound to you, so that in all things at all times, having all that you need, you will abound in every good work. . . Now he who supplies seed to the sower and bread for food will also supply and increase your store of seed and will enlarge the harvest of your righteousness. You will be made rich in every way so that you can be generous on every occasion, and through us your generosity will result in thanksgiving to God.* (2 Corinthians 9:8-11)

The richness of our healing, our caring and our sharing is built on *listening* – to God first and foremost, to others and to ourselves. In the weeks, months and years to come, may God bless your efforts as you practice what you have learned.

Other Growth Opportunities Available Through Equipping Ministries International

Apples of Gold II: Speaking the Truth in Love, explains how you can. . .

- *Move from insight to positive action.*
- *Ask questions that encourage self-understanding.*
- *Self-disclose while keeping the focus on the Seeker.*
- *Set appropriate goals and act on them.*
- *Confront effectively.*
- *Respond to inappropriate behavior.*
- *Resolve conflicts.*

Apples of Gold for Couples courses present healthy relationship building skills for married and engaged couples. They focus on creative problem-solving, emotional intimacy and couple communication.

Rational Christian Thinking teaches participants how to renew their minds and emotions. This course is helpful in overcoming anxiety, depression, stress and negative habits by replacing destructive thinking patterns with positive Scriptural truth.

Christian Family Systems teaches how to build on the strengths of an individual's family background and to overcome dysfunctional family patterns and roles. Students also learn how to help their church family become healthier and more vital.

Breaking Free From the Past is designed to help lay people and professionals find greater healing and renewal through focused prayer therapy. Presented as a small group experience, this course requires some pre-work and prerequisite courses.

Theology of a Caring, Equipping Community shows the integration of all these courses in a church or ministry setting. It presents a systematic approach to equipping and healing the growing Body of Christ.

If you'd like more information about any of our LIFE Seminars, feel free to phone our Cincinnati offices at (513) 769-5353. We'll be happy to discuss our offerings in more detail and/or send you more information about specific training opportunities held both in this country and around the world.

Professional Therapy

If you think that you or anyone you know might benefit from individual professional counseling based on solid Christian principles, you will be excited to hear that Dr. Sweeten has founded a unique professional counseling program called Life Way.

Life Way provides a full range of counseling and mental health services, including inpatient and outpatient treatment grounded in a firm commitment to Christ. The Life Way program welcomes individuals of all ages and backgrounds and is committed to helping all of God's children enjoy and celebrate life — in all its abundance.

If you're interested in Life Way's services, please phone them at (513) 769-4600 or 1-800-334-8973. They will also be happy to make referrals to our professional colleagues around the country who share their spirit and commitment.

NOTES

Preface

1. *Children's Well-Being: An International Comparison* (U. S. Department of Commerce, Bureau of the Census, November, 1989).
2. Gary R. Sweeten, *The Development of a Systematic Human Relations Training Model for Evangelical Christians*, Ed. D. Dissertation (University of Cincinnati, May, 1975).
3. Gary R. Sweeten, *Christian Care & Counsel: Apples of Gold II: Speaking the Truth in Love* (Cincinnati: Equipping Ministries International, Inc., 1987).
4. Alice Petersen, Gary R. Sweeten and Dorothy Faye Geverdt, *Rational Christian Thinking* (Cincinnati: Equipping Ministries International, Inc., 1986).
5. Gary R. Sweeten, *Breaking Free From The Past* (Cincinnati: Equipping Ministries International, Inc., 1980).
6. Gary R. Sweeten, *Christian Care & Counsel: Growing As A Christian Family* (Cincinnati: Equipping Ministries International, Inc., 1993).
7. Gary R. Sweeten, *Apples of Gold* (Cincinnati: Christian Information Committee, Inc., 1981).

Chapter 1

1. Ronald F. Inglehart, "What Is Happiness?" *USA Today,* April, 1988.

2. Margaret J. Rinck, *Can Christians Love Too Much?* (Grand Rapids, Michigan: Zondervan Publishing House, 1989).

Chapter 2

1. *The American Heritage Dictionary* (New York: American Heritage Publishing Co., Inc., 1982, 1985).
2. Gary R. Sweeten, *The Theology of a Caring, Equipping Community* (Cincinnati: Equipping Ministries International, Inc., 1992).

Chapter 3

1. P. D. Eastman, *Are You My Mother?* (New York: Beginner Books, A Division of Random House, Inc., 1960).
2. Thomas Anthony *Harris, "Im OK, You're OK* (New York: Harper & Row, 1969).
3. Wayne W. Dyer, *Pulling Your Own Strings*, (New York: Funk & Wagnalls, 1978).
4. J. I. Packer, *Knowing God* (Downers Grove, Illinois: Intervarsity Press, 1973).
5. Petersen, Sweeten and Geverdt, *Rational Christian Thinking.*
6. *Ibid.*

Chapter 6

1. Robert R. Carkhuff, *Helping and Human Relations, Volume I; Selection and Training, Volume II. Research* (New York: Holt Rinehart and Winston, 1969).
2. Gerard Egan, *The Skilled Helper*, 1975, and *Interpersonal Living*, 1976 (Brooks/Cole).

183

3. Richard Walters, *Amity, Boldness*, and other training materials (First Presbyterian Church, Boulder, Colorado).
4. Petersen, Sweeten and Geverdt, *Rational Christian Thinking*.

Chapter 7

1. Bert Decker, *The Art of Communication* (Los Altos, California: Crisp Publications, Inc., 1988).
2. Carkhuff, *Helping and Human Relations*.
3. Gary Collins, *How to Be A People Helper* (Vision House Publishers, 1976).
4. Laura S. Smark, "Adolescent Substance Use and Perceived Family Functioning," *The Journal of Family Issues*, June, 1990.
5. George and Lorene Kawash, "Self-Esteem in Early Adolescence as a Function of Position Within Olson's Circumplex Model of Marital and Family Systems," Social *Behavior and Personality*, Volume 18, 1990.
6. Deborah F. Greenwald, "Family Interaction and Child Outcome in a High-Risk Sample," *Psychological Reports*, April, 1990.
7. *Childhood Education Journal*, Winter, 1988.
8. Bernhard Wolf, "The Construct of Emotional Dedication of Kindergarten Teachers" ("Zum Konstrukt der emotionalen Zuwendung von Erzieherinnen im Kindergarten"), *Psychologie-in-Erziehung-und-Unterricht*, Volume 34, 1987.
9. Nancy Austin, "The Subtle Signs of Success," *Working Woman*, April, 1991.
10. Decker, *The Art of Communication*.
11. *Ibid.*
12. Daniel Quinn, "Lyin' Eyes," Study on *Eye Contact and Deceit*, Ohio State University.
13. Decker, *The Art of Communication*.
14. Donna Larcen, "Unwritten Rules Put Squeeze on Hugging in Business World," The Cincinnati *Enquirer,* June 22, 1991.
15. Kathleen Keating, *The Hug Therapy Book* (Minneapolis: CompCare Publishers, 1983).
16. Virginia Satir, *Peoplemaking (* Palo Alto, California: Science and Behavior Books, 1972).
17. Larcen, "Unwritten Rules Put Squeeze on Hugging in Business World. "
18. Carkhuff, *Helping and Human Relations*.

Chapter 9

1. Petersen, Sweeten and Geverdt, *Rational Christian Thinking*.
2. Sweeten, *Breaking Free*.
3. C. S. Lewis, *The Weight of Glory*, Grand Rapids, Michigan: William B. Eerdmans Publishing Company, 1979.
4. Carkhuff, *Helping and Human Relations*.
5. Annie Gottlieb, "To Love, Honor and Respect," *McCalls*, April, 1986.
6. Julius Segal, "Honor Thy Children," *Parents,* December, 1989.
7. Ruth J. Moss, "Prejudicial Esteem (Correlation of Low Self Esteem With Prejudice; Study by Jennifer Crocker and Ian Schwartz)," *Psychology Today,* September 1986.
8. John Braid and Warren Smith, "Communication Vital to Customer Satisfaction," *Cincinnati Business Courier,* August 5-11, 1991.

Notes

Chapter 10

1. William Oncken, Jr. and Donald L. Wass, "Management Time: Who's Got the Monkey?" *Harvard Business Review*, November-December, 1974.
2. Claudia Black, *It Will Never Happen to Me* (New York: Ballantine Books, 1981).
3. Robin Norwood, *Women Who Love Too Much* (Los Angeles: Jeremy Tarcher, Inc., 1985).
4. Rinck, *Can Christians Love Too Much?*
5. *Ibid.*
6. Glenbeigh Adolescent Hospital, Cleveland, Ohio as submitted by Gail Ellis, Lakewood Presbyterian Church, Lakewood, Ohio.
7. Sweeten, *Breaking Free.*

Chapter 11

1. Paul Brand and Phillip Yancey, *Fearfully and Wonderfully Made* (Grand Rapids, Michigan: Zondervan Publishing House, 1980).
2. Paul Brand and Phillip Yancy, *In His Image* (Grand Rapids, Michigan: Zondervan Publishing House, 1984).
3. *Ibid.*
4. Peggy Benson, *Listening For a God Who Whispers* (Nashville: Generoux Nelson, 1991).

Chapter 12

1. *The Cutting Edge*, Film by Paul M. Glaser, MGM/Interscope Communications, 1992.
2. Joseph Luft, *Group Processes* (Mountainview, California: Mayfield Publishers, 1984).

185

Other books and Materials in the Apples of Gold Series

The following books and materials can be ordered by phoning (513) 769-5353:

Listening for Heaven's Sake
>Leader's Manual (available 1/1/94)
>Participant Workbook

Rational Christian Thinking
>Leader's Manual

Apples of Gold II: How to Speak the Truth in Love
>Leader's Manual

Tapes Available Through Equipping Ministries International

Adult Children of Alcoholics, Sandra Wilson, Ph. D.

Counseling for Depression, Beavers, Ph. D. and Cooper, M.D., Ph. D.

From Infideliy to Love, Steve Judah, Ph. D.

Breaking Behavioral Bondage, Doug Reed, Ph. D.

Learning To Embrace Your Imperfect Self, Ken Beavers, Ph. D.

Breaking the Power of Cults, Paul R. Martin, Ph. D.

The 12 Steps of Wholeness, Sweeten, Ed. D.; Schell, M. A., Griebling, M. S.; Legender, CCDC III; Breuer, M. Ed.,CCDC III; Baker, B.A., L.S.W., L.P.C.C.

Self Esteem Redeemed, Ken Beavers, Ph. D.

(New tapes are added regularly. To get an updated list, phone Equipping Ministries International.)

Suggested Readings

The following books can be purchased through Equipping Ministries International or through your favorite Christian Bookstore:

Kenneth A. Beavers, *A Self-Esteem Guidebook* (Columbus, Ohio: Galloway Press, 1992).

David E. Carlson, *Counseling and Self-Esteem* (Waco, Texas: Word Books, 1988).

Gary Collins, *How To Be a People Helper* (Santa Ana, CA: Vision House, 1976).

John W. Cooper, *Body, Soul & Life Everlasting* (Grand Rapids, MI: William B. Eerdmans Publishing Company, 1989).

Larry Crabb, *Inside Out* (Colorado Springs: NavPress, 1988).

Tom Marshall, *Right Relationships* (Chichester, England: Sovereign World, 1989).

Alan Loy McGinnis, *The Friendship Factor* (Minneapolis: Augsburg Publishing House, 1979).

Bruce Narramore, *You're Someone Special* (Grand Rapids: Zondervan Publishing House, 1978).

Bob and Gretchen Passantino, *Witch Hunt* (Nashville: Thomas Nelson, Inc., 1990).

The 12 Steps – A Spiritual Journey (San Diego: Recovery Publications, 1988).

Dr. Ron Rand, *For Fathers Who Aren't In Heaven* (Ventura, CA: Regal Books, 1986).

Margaret J. Rinck, Ed. D., *Can Christians Love Too Much?* (Grand Rapids, MI: Zondervan Publishing House, 1989).

Margaret J. Rinck, Ed. D., *Christian Men Who Hate Women* (Grand Rapids, MI: Zondervan Publishing House, 1990).

David Semands, *Healing for Damaged Emotions* (Wheaton, IL: SP Publications, 1981).

David A. Seamands, *Putting Away Childish Things* (Wheaton, IL: SP Publications, 1982).

Steve Sjogren, *Conspiracy of Kindness* (Ann Arbor, MI: Vinebooks Servant Publications, 1993).

Melvin J. Steinbron, *Can The Pastor Do It Alone?* (Ventura, CA: Regal Books,1987).

Siang-Yang Tan, *Lay Counseling* (Grand Rapids, MI: Zondervan Publishing House, 1990).

Ruth McRoberts Ward, *Self-Esteem, Gift from God* (Grand Rapids: Baker Book House, 1984).

William P. Wilson, M.D., *The Grace to Grow* (Waco, TX: Word Books, 1984).

Sandra Wilson, Ph.D. & Gary Collins, Ph. D., *Counseling Adult Children of Alcoholics* (Dallas: Word Publishing, 1989).

Sandra Wilson, *Released From Shame* (Downers Grove, IL: Inter-Varsity Press, 1990).

Index

189

M

Manipulation 124, 130
Marriage 129
Mental 19
Mental Health 11
Miss Bumper Sticker 63
Modeling 4
Monkeys 135-152
Mt. Sunflower 67

N

Natural Revelation 14
Need-aholics 146
Nonverbal Villains 90
Nonverbals 84-89, 92-94, 117, 118

O

Obedience 36
Openness 92, 93
Over-identification 53, 54, 103, 115
Overfunctioning 147

P

Paraclete 150
paraklesis 2, 3
Paraphrasing 111-113
Parental Warmth 88
Partiality 124
Perfectionism 28
Phileo 87, 89
Phortion 141
Physical 12, 19
Physical Barriers 97
Physical Development 88
Power 30
Practice 131
Pray 131
Prejudice 129
Problem Ownership 142, 131, 145
Problem-solving 137
Problems of Feeling 47
Problems of Fellowship 47
Problems of Focus 47, 48
Professional Therapy 182
Progressive Sanctification 21
Proportional Helping 79
Psychology 12
Pupilometer 127

Q

Quadruple Type A Behavior 138
Questions 118, 119

R

RADAR Listening 103, 107-109, 115
Rational Christian Thinking
    x, 44, 75, 181
Rationalization 28
Rebellion 22
Receiving the Word of God 139
Red Light 72, 73, 75, 76, 79, 81
Redemption 41
Reflection 3
Reflective Listening 102-104, 107-109
Reinforcement 172
Relaxation 92, 95
Relax 139
Relinquish 139
Repentance 30
Resembling Our Maker 34
Resistance 170
Respect 71-73, 79, 82, 86, 103,
    123, 124, 129, 130, 132, 150
Respectability 123
Respectometer 133
Responding 139
Responsibility 150
Rhema 155, 162-165
Rx for Recovery of Serenity 139

S

Salvation Prayer 21
Sarcasm 132
Science 157
Secrecy 30
Seeker 68, 70, 72, 79, 103, 105,
107, 108, 111, 117, 171, 176
Self-awareness 119
Self-condemnation 43
Self-disclosure 71, 72
Self-esteem 34, 38-44, 88, 125,
    127, 130
Self-exploration 117
Self-image 33, 38, 41
Self-improvement 149
Self-responsibility 131
Self-understanding 72

Nonverbal Warmth

Remember:	Also consider:
S - *Sensitive Seating*	T - *Touch*
O - *Openness*	E - *Environment*
L - *Leaning*	A - *Accomodating Attitude*
A - *Appropriate Eye Contact*	
R - *Relax*	

Basic RADAR Listening Formula

Tentative Opening	+	Feeling	+	About/Because/when	+	Thought
It sounds like . . .		you feel mad. . .		about. . .		paying higher taxes.
I hear you saying that. . .		you feel sad. . .		because of. . .		what she said to you.
If I hear you correctly. . .		you feel glad. . .		when. . .		your sister succeeds.
You seem to be saying. . .		you feel afraid. . .		about. . .		your father's ill health.
I think I hear you saying. . .		you feel confused. . .		because of. . .		all the different options.
I'm not sure I'm following. . .		you feel ashamed. . .		about. . .		wanting to leave home?
Am I hearing you say. . .		you feel lonely. . .		when. . .		you remember your wife?

Feeling Words:

Mad	Sad	Glad	Afraid	Confused	Ashamed	Lonely
Bothered	Down	At Ease	Uneasy	Curious	Uncomfortable	Out of place
Ruffled	Blue	Secure	Apprehensive	Uncertain	Awkward	Left-out
Irritated	Somber	Comfortable	Careful	Ambivalent	Clumsy	Unheeded
Displeased	Low	Relaxed	Cautious	Doubtful	Self-Conscious	Lonesome
Annoyed	Glum	Contented	Hesitant	Unsettled	Disconcerted	Disconnected
Steamed	Lonely	Optimistic	Tense	Hesitant	Chagrined	Remote
Irked	Disappointed	Satisfied	Anxious	Perplexed	Abashed	Invisible
Perturbed	Worn Out	Refreshed	Nervous	Puzzled	Embarrassed	Unwelcome
Frustrated	Melancholy	Stimulated	Edgy	Muddled	Flustered	Cut-off
Angry	Downhearted	Pleased	Distressed	Distracted	Sorry	Excluded
Fed Up	Unhappy	Warm	Scared	Flustered	Apologetic	Insignificant
Disgusted	Dissatisfied	Snug	Frightened	Jumbled	Ashamed	Ignored
Indignant	Gloomy	Happy	Repulsed	Unfocused	Regretful	Neglected
Ticked Off	Mournful	Encouraged	Agitated	Fragmented	Remorseful	Separated
Bristling	Grieved	Tickled	Afraid	Dismayed	Guilty	Removed
Fuming	Depressed	Proud	Shocked	Insecure	Disgusted	Detached
Explosive	Lousy	Cheerful	Alarmed	Dazed	Belittled	Isolated
Enraged	Crushed	Thrilled	Overwhelmed	Bewildered	Humiliated	Unwanted
Irate	Defeated	Delighted	Frantic	Lost	Violated	Rejected
Incensed	Dejected	Joyful	Panic Stricken	Stunned	Dirty	Deserted
Burned	Empty	Elated	Horrified	Chaotic	Mortified	Outcast
Burned Up	Wretched	Exhilarated	Petrified	Torn	Defiled	Abandoned
Outraged	Despairing	Overjoyed	Terrified	Baffled	Devastated	Desolate
Furious	Devastated	Ecstatic	Numb	Dumbfounded	Degraded	Forsaken

(Each feeling-word column is marked with a gradient scale from "A Little" at the top to "A Lot" at the bottom.)

193